McGRAW-HILL LANGUAGE ARTS

Language Support

Grade 6 Lessons/Practice/Blackline Masters

**McGraw-Hill
School Division**

New York   Farmington

Table of Contents

Grade 6

Unit 4: Adjectives and Expository Writing

Unit 5: Pronouns and Story Writing

Unit 6: Adverbs, Prepositions, Interjections and Persuasive Writing

Meeting the Needs of Second-Language Learners with McGraw-Hill Language Arts

McGraw-Hill Language Arts is dedicated to making all students, including second-language learners, effective communicators. The Teacher's Editions at each grade level provide point-of-use suggestions to encourage the participation of second-language learners in each lesson. This Language Support Handbook expands on those suggestions with strategies and activities designed to help you move second-language learners through the stages of language acquisition and prepare them for success in the mainstream language arts curriculum.

Features of the Second-Language Acquisition Program

A language-rich, risk-free setting

The Natural Approach to Language Learning Most people learn to speak fluently by listening, imitating, and trying out a new language. McGraw-Hill Language Arts, through this Language Support Handbook, maximizes this experience by making the classroom a language-rich, risk-free setting where students experiment with language in various contexts. By creating an environment where there is a real need to communicate, the program allows students to produce more language and to make great strides toward fluency.

Whole class instruction around the same theme

Thematic Units The program uses themes to create the context which makes language content meaningful and accessible. In each grade, vocabulary, concepts, and language skills are developed across six themes. Because instruction for the whole class is planned around the same theme or concept, inclusion of and appropriate instruction for second-language learners are ensured.

Meet needs at different levels

Multilevel Strategies Each lesson in this Language Support Handbook provides teaching strategies for students at various proficiency levels. Organized to parallel the mainstream language arts curriculum for each grade level, the multilevel learning activities allow all students access to grade-level content.

Bring out the best in every learner

Variety of Instructional Groupings To bring out the best in all learners, the program uses a variety of instructional groupings: (a) pairs— new English learners are paired with more proficient speakers; (b) small groups—students at all proficiency levels work together; (c) individual interaction with tutors, partners, teaching assistants, and parents; and (d) whole class activities.

Make use of informal assessment opportunities

Appropriate Assessment This Language Support Handbook provides for ongoing evaluation where the processes and products of students' work serve as the basis for assessment. Evaluation strategies include using teacher observations and interactions as a basis for assessment, allowing students to perform an activity that will show the application of a concept, and evaluating progress through student portfolios.

Communicating in Every Way

To promote understanding of messages necessary to acquire language, the language support program enables you to cover concepts using a variety of sensory input such as gestures, pictures, graphic organizers, demonstrations, role-plays, pantomime, and variations in pitch and tone of voice. Activities that require total physical response (TPR) are indicated throughout this Language Support Handbook.

Multi-sensory input

Total Physical Response TPR is a well-established and successful technique that links language to a physical response. The classic game of "Simon Says" is a vivid example. The teacher (or a student) can call out a series of commands (i.e., "Simon says, raise your arms") and students respond with the appropriate physical gesture—in this case, by raising their arms. The advantage of this technique is it links language to the "here and now," giving second-language learners, especially at the early stages, a concrete forum for language practice. As your students continue to use TPR and their oral proficiency increases, you will find that they will naturally rely less and less on the technique. Until that point is reached, however, TPR will engage your second-language learners, build their vocabulary, and encourage them to develop and improve the oral language skills they need to master in order to achieve full English proficiency.

Concrete forum for language practice

Examples of Appropriate TPR Commands

Stand up	Giggle	Turn your head to the right
Sit down	Make a face	Drum your fingers
Touch the floor	Flex your muscles	Wet your lips
Raise your arm	Wave to me	Blow a kiss
Put down your arm	Shrug your shoulders	Cough
Pat your cheek	Tickle your side	Sneeze
Wipe your face	Clap your hands	Shout "help"
Scratch your knee	Point to the ceiling	Spell your name
Massage your neck	Cry	Laugh
Stretch	Yawn	Sing
Whisper (a word)	Hum	Hop on one foot
Step forward	Lean backwards	Make a fist
Shake your hand	(Name), walk to the door	(Name), turn on the lights

Source: Richard-Amato, P. (1996). Making it happen: Interaction in the second-language classroom, 2nd ed. White Plains, N.Y.: Addison-Wesley Publishing Group/Longman

Stages of Second-Language Acquisition

Second-language learners move through a series of predictable stages as they make strides toward fluency. The following chart was designed to provide you with a set of reasonable expectations and appropriate teaching approaches to meet the unique needs of students at each language proficiency level.

Stages	Students are able to:	Appropriate teaching approaches include:
1 **Pre-Production**	• understand broad concepts and the gist of conversation • extract meaning from multi-sensory clues such as gestures and visuals • respond non-verbally by drawing and acting out vocabulary, concepts, and events • transfer acquired skills from their first-language learning experience • apply prior knowledge to their current classroom experience • gain greater familiarity with the sounds and patterns of English by listening actively to speakers and audio/video recordings of various contexts	• building on prior knowledge and existing skills developed in the first language • modeling tasks and giving examples • providing opportunities for active listening through dialogue, read-alouds, choral reading, and audio/visual presentations • providing visual support for oral and written messages, such as with realia, manipulatives, and illustrations • allowing students to use total physical response to participate in language activities • encouraging nonverbal expressions, such as mime, art, music, and dance • lavishing praise for all attempts to communicate
2 **Early Production**	• understand much more of what is being said • begin repeating and producing English words, phrases, and simple sentences • understand and use greetings and common expressions with confidence • show some reading comprehension if illustrations are present • demonstrate identification and classification of people, places, and things • begin framing questions to clarify meaning or request more information	• presenting the lesson in the context of students' personal experiences • modeling expected short responses to verbal or written prompts • asking questions that require one- or two-word responses • providing visual support for oral and written messages, such as with realia, manipulatives, and illustrations • providing opportunities for students to create labels and captions for objects and pictures • providing an experiential environment in which students may freely engage in active listening and speaking • encouraging all forms of creative expression such as mime, art, music, and dance • allowing students sufficient time to hear, think, and formulate responses • lavishing praise for every risk taken

Stages	Students are able to:	Appropriate teaching approaches include:
3 **Speech Emergence**	• demonstrate increased comprehension of spoken English • respond in longer phrases or sentences with less hesitation • understand oral and written communication about personal experiences • discuss everyday events, the past, and some future personal events • incorporate content area concepts in oral and written expression • begin to read English without accompanying illustrations • work with less supervision, using previously learned routines	• modeling correct language forms after accepting responses • asking open-ended questions that require short answers and higher-level thinking skills • providing oral and written activities that validate students' cultural identities • using heterogeneous groupings to enable students of different abilities to assist one another (peer tutoring) • providing opportunities for oral and written expression for different purposes and audiences • exposing students to a variety of content-area experiences • gently allowing students silent periods and lapses of decreased correctness as they assimilate new material • lavishing praise for every risk taken
4, 5 **Intermediate and Advanced Fluency**	• understand oral and written communication involving more abstract themes • converse with varied grammatical structures and more extensive vocabulary • express thoughts and feelings with fluency • demonstrate skills in persuading, evaluating, justifying, and elaborating • engage in debates and discuss "what-if" situations • write for different audiences and purposes while demonstrating increased levels of accuracy and correctness • work independently on their own instructional level (At stage 5, students are able to use extensive vocabulary and complex grammatical structures in much the same way as their native English-speaking peers.)	• modeling correct English language patterns and structures after accepting responses • asking open-ended questions that require more detailed answers and higher-level thinking skills • focusing on oral and written communication that requires higher-order language such as persuasion, analysis, and evaluation • allowing students to discuss and model learning strategies • using a variety of instructional groupings to bring out the best in every learner and create opportunities for peer tutoring • integrating language arts and content-area learning experiences • providing opportunities for more abstract oral and written expression for a variety of purposes and audiences

Scope and Sequence

Oral Language Development

All students in grade 6 are expected to:	Teaching approaches to help second language learners at each stage meet expectations include the following:
<ul><li>respond appropriately to oral communications</li><li>ask thoughtful questions</li><li>identify how language usage reflects regional and cultural differences</li><li>recite brief poems, dramatic dialogues, using clear diction, tempo, volume, and phrasing</li><li>deliver oral summaries of articles and books</li><li>make narrative and informational presentations</li><li>provide a context for listeners to imagine an event or experience</li><li>emphasize points that make clear to viewers and listeners the important ideas and concepts</li><li>give precise directions and instructions</li><li>incorporate more than one source of information</li><li>employ details, anecdotes, examples, volume, pitch, phrasing, pace modulation, and gestures to explain, clarify, or enhance meaning</li><li>use traditional structures for putting together information</li><li>evaluate the role of the news media in focusing attention on events and in forming opinions about them</li></ul>	**Stage 1: Pre-Production**<ul><li>modeling of verbal prompts by gesturing, role-playing, pantomiming</li><li>pointing to pictures or real objects to demonstrate meanings</li><li>encouraging students to respond in nonverbal ways</li><li>providing a risk-free environment where any kind of speech production is welcomed but not required</li></ul>**Stage 2: Early Production**<ul><li>building on existing oral language skills</li><li>asking *yes/no*, *either/or*, and simple questions that require one- or two-word responses</li><li>simplifying, restating, repeating and demonstrating verbal and written prompts</li><li>encouraging the use of TPR (Total Physical Response) to demonstrate understanding</li><li>providing activities that allow students to manipulate or label real objects or pictures</li><li>allowing for some participation in paired or small-group speaking and listening activities</li><li>motivating students to take risks with language</li></ul>**Stage 3: Speech Emergence**<ul><li>providing meaningful contexts where students can express themselves orally</li><li>asking open-ended questions that require short responses and higher-level thinking skills</li><li>drawing analogies to students' personal experiences to explain culturally unfamiliar topics</li><li>allowing sufficient time for students to hear, think, and formulate responses</li><li>accepting students' oral responses even if they are not grammatically correct and use unvaried sentence structure</li><li>setting up heterogeneous groups to give modeling of spoken English a natural context</li></ul>**Stages 4 and 5: Intermediate and Advanced Fluency**<ul><li>modeling correct oral language conventions</li><li>asking open-ended questions that require detailed responses and higher-level thinking skills</li><li>creating realistic contexts for debates, discussion of "what-if" situations, and elaboration of ideas</li><li>providing speaking and listening activities that allow students to analyze, compare and contrast, and make generalizations</li><li>assigning the same oral language activities given to the mainstream class, rephrasing and clarifying directions as needed</li></ul>

Language Patterns and Structures

All students in grade 6 are expected to exhibit understanding of:	Teaching approaches to help second language learners at each stage meet expectations include the following:

All students in grade 6 are expected to exhibit understanding of:

- Sentences and Sentence Fragments
- Kinds of Sentences
- Combining Sentences: Complex Sentences
- Combining Sentences: Compound Subjects and Predicates
- Singular and Plural Nouns
- More Plural Nouns
- Common and Proper Nouns
- Possessive Nouns
- Verb Tenses
- Subject-Verb Agreement
- Progressive Forms
- Irregular Verbs
- Adjectives
- Comparative and Superlative Adjectives
- Comparing with *More* and *Most, Good* and *Bad*
- Pronouns and Referents
- Subject and Object Pronouns
- Indefinite Pronouns
- Adverbs that Modify Verbs
- Adverbs that Modify Adjectives and Adverbs
- Prepositions
- Prepositional Phrases

Teaching approaches to help second language learners at each stage meet expectations include the following:

Stage 1: Pre-Production
- supplementing verbal and written prompts with gestures, pantomime, and role-playing
- using realia or manipulatives to demonstrate meanings
- encouraging nonverbal responses to multi-sensory stimuli
- allowing for silent periods during which students internally rehearse the sounds, words, and phrases that are silently becoming part of their new language

Stage 2: Early Production
- using prior language skills as springboards to teach new language patterns
- allowing one- or two-word responses to simple questions
- clarifying verbal and written prompts by simplifying, restating, and demonstrating
- using appropriate TPR (Total Physical Response) commands
- enabling students to manipulate or label real objects or pictures
- using a variety of instructional groupings
- motivating students to take risks with language

Stage 3: Speech Emergence
- putting language patterns in meaningful contexts
- enabling students to use higher-level thinking skills, but requiring short responses to questions
- drawing analogies to students' personal experiences to explain culturally unfamiliar structures and patterns
- allowing sufficient time for students to hear, think, and formulate responses
- focusing on correct content, not on grammatical errors
- encouraging students to assimilate and apply correct English language structures and patterns in heterogeneous group activities

Stages 4 and 5: Intermediate and Advanced Fluency
- modeling correct English language patterns and structures
- enabling students to use higher-level thinking skills, and requiring detailed responses to questions
- creating realistic contexts for using correct grammar and sentence structures
- providing activities that allow students to use varied grammatical structures and more extensive vocabulary
- encouraging full participation in mainstream learning activities

Scope and Sequence

Vocabulary, Composition, and Study Skills

All students in grade 6 are expected to exhibit understanding of skills and concepts in each area.

Teaching approaches to help second language learners at each stage meet expectations include the following:

Vocabulary Skills

- Time-Order Words

- How Language Changes

- Prefixes and Suffixes

- Synonyms and Antonyms

- Root Words

- Word Choice

Composition Skills

- Main Idea

- Outlining

- Organization

- Writing Descriptions

- Writing Dialogue

- Leads and Endings

Study Skills

- Look Up Words in a Dictionary

- Use Parts of a Book

- Use an Encyclopedia

- Card Catalog at the Library or Media Center

- Note-taking While Watching a Documentary

- On-line Search

Stage 1: Pre-Production

- showing real objects or large visuals to make academic content comprehensible
- linking sounds to pictures and pictures to sounds
- using gestures, pantomime, or role-playing to demonstrate concepts and tasks
- encouraging nonverbal participation in learning activities
- providing ample opportunities for students to absorb the language-rich environment in the classroom

Stage 2: Early Production

- building on prior knowledge to develop new skills and concepts
- asking questions that require predictable one- or two-word responses
- simplifying, restating, repeating, and demonstrating verbal and written prompts
- encouraging the use of TPR (Total Physical Response) to demonstrate understanding
- providing activities that allow students to manipulate or label real objects or pictures
- allowing for some participation in paired or small-group activities
- motivating students to take risks with new vocabulary and strategies

Stage 3: Speech Emergence

- providing meaningful contexts where students can apply vocabulary, composition, and study skills
- asking open-ended questions that require short responses and higher-level thinking skills
- drawing analogies to students' personal experiences to explain culturally unfamiliar content
- allowing sufficient time for students to hear, think, and formulate responses
- setting up heterogeneous groups to enable students to learn from their peers

Stages 4 and 5: Intermediate and Advanced Fluency

- modeling correct use of new vocabulary, composition, or study skills
- asking open-ended questions that require detailed responses and higher-level thinking skills
- providing activities that allow students to use more extensive vocabulary
- creating realistic contexts for using reference materials
- assigning the same practice exercises given to the mainstream class, rephrasing and clarifying directions as needed

Writing Skills

All students in grade 6 are expected to:	Teaching approaches to help second language learners at each stage meet expectations include the following:

All students in grade 6 are expected to:

- **write for a different purpose/audience**
  - write to inform
  - write to explain
  - write to entertain
  - write to persuade
  - write to express, discover, record, reflect on ideas, and problem solve

- **write in different modes**
  - personal narrative
  - writing that compares
  - explanatory (how-to) writing
  - expository writing
  - story writing
  - persuasive writing

- **write using a variety of forms**
  - book reviews, friendly and business letters, thank-you notes, postcards, invitations, e-mail messages, news or magazine articles, newscasts, weather reports, comic strips, posters, postcards, journal entries, instructions, essays, biographies, stories, plays, poems, captions, announcements, travel brochures

- **apply writing processes**
  - prewriting
  - research and inquiry
  - drafting
  - revising
  - proofreading
  - publishing

Teaching approaches to help second language learners at each stage meet expectations include the following:

Stage 1: Pre-Production
- modeling of tasks by gesturing, role-playing, pantomiming
- using pictures or real objects to demonstrate meanings
- encouraging students to respond in nonverbal ways
- creating a risk-free setting where any kind of written production is welcomed but not required

Stage 2: Early Production
- building on existing writing skills
- simplifying, restating, repeating and demonstrating writing prompts
- using appropriate TPR (Total Physical Response) commands to provide a concrete forum for language practice
- encourage language production while students manipulate or label real objects or pictures
- allowing for some participation in paired or small-group writing activities
- motivating students to take risks with writing

Stage 3: Speech Emergence
- providing meaningful contexts where students can express themselves in writing
- requiring short written responses using higher-level thinking skills
- drawing analogies to students' personal experiences to explain culturally unfamiliar topics
- allowing sufficient time for students to hear, think, and formulate written compositions
- setting up heterogeneous groups to allow students to learn from one another

Stages 4 and 5: Intermediate and Advanced Fluency
- modeling correct English writing conventions
- creating realistic contexts for written communication
- providing writing activities that allow students to narrate, explain, persuade, analyze, compare and contrast, and make generalizations
- encouraging active participation in mainstream learning activities

Addressing Specific Problems

A student at the pre-production level seems withdrawn and won't say a word.

> Students at the pre-production stage of language acquisition normally go through a silent period during which they are internally transferring learned skills from their first language and prior academic experience. They are absorbing the language-rich environment of your classroom.

A student at the early production level is often hesitant to speak in class.

> If silence is habitual, it might be a result of lack of self-confidence or an issue about risk-taking or appropriateness. Many factors, such as culture, gender, personality, and personal experience, influence an individual's perception of acceptable risk or appropriateness. Provide a risk-free environment in which participation is welcomed but not mandated.

A student at the speech emergence level is suddenly hesitant to participate and makes careless grammatical errors when he or she does answer.

> Brief silent periods often signal that new vocabulary and language patterns are being internally rehearsed and learned. Resume oral prompts with volunteers while you wait for the student to either volunteer an answer or request clarification. If, when the student does speak, his or her grammar isn't perfect, that is understandable. Focus instead on whether the new material is being assimilated correctly and commend him or her for a job well done.

A new student has trouble transitioning from drawing to writing text for written assignments and also has difficulty reading.

> Consider the differences between English and the student's first language. Does it use a different alphabet? Is the text read from left to right or from right to left? Naturally, reading and writing a completely different language takes a great deal of patience and encouragement.

A student who has no trouble with conversational English demonstrates below-average performance in academic contexts.

> Academic language proficiency develops much later, often not until the fourth or fifth stage of language acquisition is achieved. To help students make giant strides toward fluency, provide comprehensible materials connected to the themes of the mainstream curriculum.

Some students can't seem to give a straight answer. Some never ask questions.

> Cultural backgrounds often come into play during classroom interactions. For instance, in some Asian cultures it is considered more polite to communicate thoughts indirectly than to be bluntly direct. In some Hispanic cultures, questioning may be viewed as disrespectful behavior as it interrupts the teacher's presentation. Be careful not to ask students to choose between the home culture and the dominant culture in the classroom. Let them observe how classmates communicate, and give them time to assimilate your preferred model for communication.

Students exhibit mixed skills, such as the oral skills of Advanced Fluency, the reading skills of Intermediate Fluency, and the writing skills of Speech Emergence.

> Second-language learners tend to exhibit ever-changing proficiency levels in listening, speaking, reading, and writing. Build on their strengths to improve on their weaknesses.

SENTENCES AND SENTENCE FRAGMENTS

I. DEVELOP ORAL LANGUAGE
Oral Focus on Grammar Skill

Objective: Orally describe photographs and identify sentences and sentence fragments.

Whole Group Oral Language Activity

Invite students to look at the photograph on page 2 of the textbook. Write the words *Sentences* and *Sentence Fragments* on the chalkboard. Ask: *What do you see here? What is in the box?* Say: *Describe what is in the box.* Ask: *What is next to the box? Who do you think wrote the card? Who is the card to? Tell me what you think will happen next.* Write student responses under the appropriate heading.

Tell the class that a *sentence* is a complete thought. Explain that complete sentences always have a subject and a predicate. The subject tells who or what the sentence is about, while the predicate tells what is happening. Invite a volunteer to point to or read aloud a sentence from your list, such as *The father puts on the tie.* Encourage them to point out the subject (the father) and the predicate (puts on the tie). Then explain that a *sentence fragment* is a group of words that is only part of a sentence; this group of words is missing either the subject or the predicate. Now invite a volunteer to point to or read aloud a sentence fragment, such as *a card* and *a tie,* from your list. Ask: *What is missing in this sentence fragment?* (the predicate) Repeat the exercise using the photograph from page 3. This time, repeat back students' answers and ask them to choose whether their answers are sentences or sentence fragments. If they have used sentence fragments, encourage them to complete the fragments to make whole sentences.

Scaffolded Verbal Prompting

Use the following verbal prompts to help students better understand sentences and sentence fragments.

Nonverbal Prompt for Active Participation

Pre-Production: *Look at the picture. Point to an object. Now show me what it is doing.*

One- or Two-Word Response Prompt

Early Production: *Name an object in the picture. Now tell me what might happen to the object.*

Prompt for Short Answers to Higher-Level Thinking Skills

Speech Emergence: *Tell me what is in the picture. What will happen next? Which words tell what is in the picture, and which words tell what is happening?*

Prompt for Detailed Answers to Higher-Level Thinking Skills

Intermediate and Advanced Fluency: *Tell me what you see. Now tell me what is happening. Next, tell me what you see and what is happening in one complete sentence. Repeat the sentence. Tell me what two sentence fragments you used to make the complete sentence.*

II. DEVELOP GRAMMAR SKILLS IN CONTEXT
Visual/Physical Focus on Grammar Skill

Objective: Develop and demonstrate understanding of sentences and sentence fragments.

Materials: Blackline Master 1, scissors, pencils

TPR

Extension: Write several sentences and sentence fragments on the chalkboard. Ask volunteers to mark an "X" next to complete sentences and an "O" next to the sentence fragments.

<u>Fragment:</u>
visited our cousins.
<u>Complete Sentence:</u>
We like Boston.

Extension: Have players say the complete sentence aloud before taking a matching pair from the set. Invite them to discuss what they know about the subject, using complete sentences.

Whole Group Activity

On one side of the chalkboard write the sentence fragment *My pen pal* and on the other side of the chalkboard write the sentence fragment *lives in Canada.* Provide each student with a copy of Blackline Master 1. Instruct students to trace the word *subject* in the upper fragment card. In the lower fragment card ask them to trace the word *predicate.* Invite students to cut out each fragment. Students then hold up the subject fragment card when they hear the sentence fragment containing the subject. Students will repeat this action with the predicate fragment card when they hear the sentence fragment containing the predicate. Finally, invite them to place the two fragment cards together and say aloud the complete sentence, *My pen pal lives in Canada.* Repeat the exercise with other sentences and sentence fragments.

Small Group Activity

Invite students to think about fun things they usually do with their family or friends. *(I go camping with my family. Malcolm and I go to art museums.)* Have students break their sentences into fragments. Then ask a volunteer to say aloud a sentence fragment, such as *went to the Black Hills.* If the sentence fragment is missing the subject, other students in the group will ask, for instance, *What do you do with your family?* The speaker will then provide the complete sentence. Similarly, if the fragment is missing the predicate *(Malcolm and I)* other students will ask, for example, *What do you and Malcolm do?* Repeat the exercise until each student in the group has had a chance to be speaker.

Partner Activity

Have partners work together to create a deck of twenty cards. Help students begin by telling them that one card should show a sentence fragment with a subject while its partner should have a sentence fragment with a matching predicate. For instance, one card may read, *My grandparents* while the other reads *live in South Dakota.* Have partners shuffle the cards then place them face down. Partners take turns turning two cards face up, looking for matching sentence fragments that make a correct complete sentence. The game ends when all the pairs are correctly matched.

Technology Link

Type a list of complete sentences and sentence fragments onto a computer screen. Have partners of varying language levels work together to create complete sentences from the sentence fragments.

III. PRACTICE GRAMMAR SKILLS
Written Focus on Grammar Skills

Use Blackline Masters 2 and 3 to reinforce distinguishing complete sentences from sentence fragments.

Introduce Blackline Master 2: A Maze of Fragments

Objective: Form complete sentences from sentence fragments.

Materials: Blackline Master 2; pencil

Explain to students that forming complete sentences is sometimes like walking through a maze; you have to keep searching till you find the right words. Divide the class into pairs of varying language levels. Distribute Blackline Master 2. Read aloud and discuss the directions with students. Explain that the correct path on the maze will lead the students to match three sets of sentence fragments, which they will write next to the appropriate illustrations. When pairs have completed their mazes, invite them to read aloud the three complete sentences to tell the story.

Informal Assessment

Have students turn to page 3 in their textbooks. Read aloud a sentence fragment from More Practice A. Ask, *Is this a complete sentence or a sentence fragment? How do you know?* Repeat the questioning with a complete sentence.

Introduce Blackline Master 3: The Complete Story

Objective: Complete sentence fragments to form logical sentences.

Materials: Blackline Master 3; pencil

Invite students to work in pairs. Distribute Blackline Master 3. Have pairs look over the sentence fragments and their accompanying illustrations. Then challenge them to complete each fragment so that it corresponds with its illustration. On the last line, invite partners to write their own complete sentence and draw an illustration, both of which will bring an end to the story they have created.

Informal Assessment

Have students turn to page 15, and point to the photo on the page. Ask, *What do you see here?* After hearing students' responses, ask, *Was your answer a complete sentence or a sentence fragment?* If it was a sentence fragment, challenge them to add words to make it a complete sentence. Repeat the exercise with other questions, such as, *What is the family doing? How do you think they are feeling?*

Use the following chart to assess and reteach.

Are students able to:	
orally describe the contents of a picture?	Reteach using Language Support Activity on TE page 2 for oral practice.
put together words to make sentences?	Reteach using MINS Reteach Blackline Master page 1.
identify sentences and sentence fragments?	Reteach using the Reteach Activity on TE page 3.

Sentence Fragments

Trace the word *subject* in the upper card. Trace the word *predicate* in the lower card. Cut out each card.

subject

Who?
What?

predicate

What
happened?

IDENTIFY KINDS OF SENTENCES

I. DEVELOP ORAL LANGUAGE
Oral focus on Grammar Skill

Objective: Orally develop knowledge of kinds of sentences through the use of visual aids.

Whole Group Oral Language Activity

Invite students to look at the photograph on page 4. Ask: *What do you see?* Write the answer under the heading, *Declarative Sentence.* Ask: *What do you want to ask about the picture?* Write the answer under the heading, *Interrogative Sentence.* Third, say: *Tell the boy what you want him to do.* Write the answer under the heading, *Imperative Sentences.* Finally, ask: *What would you yell?* Write the answer under the heading, *Exclamatory Sentence.*

Tell the class that they have just used four different kinds of sentences. Explain that a declarative sentence makes a statement and ends with a period. Have a volunteer use a declarative sentence about the photograph on page 5. *(The girl is smiling.)* Next, explain that an interrogative sentence asks a question and ends with a question mark. Have someone make an interrogative sentence about the photo. *(What is the girl lying on?)* Explain that an imperative sentence makes a command or request. Ask a volunteer to request the girl to do something. *(Please share your sled with me.)* Then explain that an exclamatory sentence expresses strong feeling and ends with an exclamation point. Ask a student to make an exclamatory sentence related to the photo. *(I love sledding!)* Repeat the exercise with magazine photos.

Scaffolded Verbal Prompting

Use the following verbal prompts to help students better understand the kinds of sentences.

Nonverbal Prompt for Active Participation

Pre-Production: *Look at the picture. Point to the person. Now show me what the boy is doing.*

One- or Two-Word Response Prompt

Early Production: *Name the person in the picture. Tell me what the boy is doing.*

Prompt for Short Answers to Higher-Level Thinking Skills

Speech Emergence: *Tell me who is in the picture. What questions do you have about the picture?*

Prompt for Detailed Answers to Higher-Level Thinking Skills

Intermediate and Advanced Fluency: *Explain what you would tell the boy in the picture to do. Repeat the sentence. What kind of sentence is it? Can you change it to a question?*

II. DEVELOP GRAMMAR SKILLS IN CONTEXT
Visual/Physical Focus on Grammar Skill

Objective: Develop and demonstrate understanding of kinds of sentences through listening.

Materials: Blackline Master 4, colors or markers, scissors

TPR

Extension: Write four kinds of sentences on the chalkboard. Ask a student to place the correct punctuation mark and label each kind of sentence.

We paint in art class
Do you like to read
Please give me the ruler
I love to play soccer

Whole Group Activity

Provide each student with a copy of Blackline Master 4. Instruct students to color in each card a certain color so that, for instance, all declarative sentences boxes are green. Have students cut out each card and lay them all out in front of them, face up. Review with students the punctuation marks used in each kind of sentence. Then say a sentence aloud, such as *I love my little sister!* Have students hold up the appropriate card. Repeat the exercise, using all four kinds of sentences several times.

Small Group Activity

Have groups of four stand in a circle. Assign them a number from 1 to 4. Explain that the ones are the declarative sentences, the twos are the interrogatory sentences, the threes are the imperative sentences, and the fours are the exclamatory sentences. Tell students to each take a turn and step into the circle, then say something about your school, using their assigned sentence types. For instance, a student might step forward and say the declarative sentence, *Our school is on Bridge Street.* Another student might say the imperative sentence, *Please help us keep our school clean.* When everyone in each circle has had a turn, rotate the kinds of sentences between groups and repeat the exercise.

Partner Activity

Invite partners to interview each other about their lives, using each kind of sentence. Provide a model such as the following. Speaker one: *Please tell me where your family is from.* Speaker two: *My family is from Brazil.* Speaker one: *Have you ever been to Brazil?* Speaker two: *I get to go this summer!* Have them use the cards from Blackline Master 1 as cue cards for reference.

Technology Link

Have students type their interviews into a computer. Tell them to include the name of each kind of sentence. Then have them print out their interview and read it aloud to the rest of the class.

III. PRACTICE GRAMMAR SKILLS
Written Focus on Grammar Skills

Use Blackline Masters 5 and 6 to help children determine when to use different types of punctuation, and what punctuation means.

Introduce Blackline Master 5: Is There a Clue? There is a Clue!

Objective: To form different kinds of sentences using their parts as clues.

Materials: Blackline Master 5; pencil

Explain to students that punctuation marks can act as clues when trying to figure out a sentence type. Divide the class into pairs of varying language levels. Distribute Blackline Master 5. Tell students to use picture and word clues to add punctuation to each sentence. Then have them draw a line between the sentences and the kind of sentence.

Informal Assessment

Have students turn to page 5 of their textbooks. Read aloud a sentence and ask: *What kind of sentence is this? How do you know?* Repeat the questioning with all four kinds of sentences.

Introduce Blackline Master 6: Fixing Up a Story

Objective: Creating sentences to make a story, using art and text clues.

Materials: Blackline Master 6; pencil

Distribute Blackline Master 6. Explain to students that the illustrations will work to help them write a short scene about what is happening. Have students look at the punctuation on each line and determine what kind of sentence will best go there. Then invite them to write a sentence for each illustration. When they are done, students can read aloud what they have written and compare their sentences with those of other students.

Informal Assessment

Have students look at a magazine picture, and say: *Tell me what you see in the photograph.* Have students ask a question about another photograph. Then, invite a student to make a request about the magazine you show them next. Finally, ask students to express strong feelings about the last photo you look over together. Each time a student says a sentence, ask the class what kind of sentence it was.

Use the following chart to assess and reteach.

Are students able to: use visual aids to develop knowledge of kinds of sentences?	Reteach using Hands-On Activity on TE page 2a.
demonstrate understanding of kinds of sentences through listening?	Reteach using Language Support activity on TE page 4.
create sentences using context clues?	Reteach using the Reteach activity on TE page 5.

Kinds of Sentences

Read the punctuation marks on each card. Cut out the four cards. Hold up the correct card when the sentence is read.

_____ •

_____ ?

Please _____ •

_____ !

COMBINING SENTENCES: COMPLEX SENTENCES

I. DEVELOP ORAL LANGUAGE
Oral Focus on Grammar Skill

Objective: Orally describe and show understanding of complex sentences through songs.

Whole Group Oral Language Activity

Teach the class the song, "If I Had a Hammer." After singing several verses and familiarizing students with the song, write down the first sentence: *If I had a hammer, I'd hammer in the morning.* Read it aloud and ask: *Is this a complete sentence?* Then cover the first clause and ask if the second clause is a complete sentence. (yes) Explain that this is called an independent clause; it can stand alone as a sentence. Cover the second clause and ask if the first clause is a complete sentence. (no) Explain that this is a dependent clause; it cannot stand alone as a sentence because it begins with the conjunction *if.* Explain that conjunctions are words that connect clauses.

Then invite children to sing the song "She'll Be Coming Around the Mountain." After singing through all the verses, write the first line: *She'll be coming around the mountain when she comes.* Repeat the exercise, pointing out that this time the second clause is the dependent clause, because it begins with the conjunction *when.* Invite students to sing the song again, clapping in unison when they hear the conjunction.

Scaffolded Verbal Prompting

Use the following verbal prompts to help students better understand complex sentences.

Nonverbal Prompt for Active Participation

Pre-Production: *Listen to the song. Clap when you hear the word* when. *Now act out the song.*

One- or Two-Word Response Prompt

Early Production: *Listen to the song. Clap and sing aloud the word* when *each time you hear it.*

Prompt for Short Answers to Higher-Level Thinking Skills

Speech Emergence: *Sing the song with me, and clap when you hear the word* when. *Tell me what is happening in the song.*

Prompt for Detailed Answers to Higher-Level Thinking Skills

Intermediate and Advanced Fluency: *Sing the song aloud. Now tell me what word joins the two parts of the sentence. Which part of the sentence cannot stand alone as a sentence? Why?*

II. DEVELOP GRAMMAR SKILLS IN CONTEXT
Visual/Physical Focus on Grammar Skill

Objective: Develop and demonstrate understanding of complex sentences.

Materials: Blackline Master 7, scissors

Whole Group Activity

Have students turn to the photograph on page 13. Invite them to tell what they see. Then invite them to talk about what they like to do on sunny days. Then model a complex sentence, using what students have told you. *(If it is sunny, Miguel likes to ride his bike. Sally plays in the backyard while her mother gardens.)* Ask volunteers to point out the conjunction, dependent and independent clauses. Distribute copies of Blackline Master 7. Copy the word box of conjunctions on the board. Have students orally describe what they see in each picture. Then have students cut out the cards. Invite a volunteer to choose two cards and create an independent and dependent clause that combines the action in the cards. Then have him or her come to the board and point to the conjunction they used to combine the sentences. Repeat with other sentences.

Small Group Activity

TPR

Extension: Write three of the sentences on the chalkboard. Ask a student to underline the dependent clause and circle the conjunction in each sentence.

I go to the river whenever it is warm out.

Unless it is raining, I always play outside.

Write the following conjunctions on the chalkboard: *after, if, whenever, unless, before, while.* Ask students to act out what they do after they get out of school. *(After I get out of school, I go to soccer practice).* As each sentence is acted out, invite one student to say aloud the complex sentence beginning with the word *after.* Ask another student to identify the dependent clause and the independent clause in the sentence. Repeat the exercise with other conjunctions. (Example: *What do you do before you go to bed? I brush my teeth before I go to bed.*)

Partner Activity

On the chalkboard, write the following conjunctions: *after, although, as, as if, as though, because, before, if, since, though, until, unless, where, wherever, whenever, while.* Have partners of varying language levels choose five of the conjunctions from which they will create complex sentences about friendships. *(Whenever Josh comes over, we play hide and seek. I like to go to Fiona's house because she has toy cars.)* Tell partners to make a poster that illustrates each of their complex sentences. When they are done with their posters, have them write its complex sentence on the bottom. Partners can then share their posters with the rest of the class.

Technology Link

Type several complex sentences on the computer screen. Challenge partners to rearrange each sentence so that the dependent clause appears in a different place. Remind students to use the cut and paste functions on the computer to facilitate their edits. Also remind them that they may need to add, delete, or change certain punctuation.

III. PRACTICE GRAMMAR SKILLS
Written Focus on Grammar Skills

Use Blackline Masters 8 and 9 to reinforce their understanding of complex sentences and how to complete them.

Introduce Blackline Master 8: When You Find the Answer . . .

Objective: To complete complex sentences using context clues.

Materials: Blackline Master 8; pencil

Distribute copies of Blackline Master 8 to students and look over the art together. Ask volunteers to describe what they see. Read aloud the directions and discuss them with students. Then invite students to fill in the correct missing conjunction in each sentence so that it matches what the art is showing.

Informal Assessment

Have students turn to page 9 in their textbooks. Read aloud the first complex sentence from More Practice A and ask volunteers to point to and say aloud the conjunction. Ask: *Would the conjunction* as though *work here? Why not? Why does the conjunction* although *work best?*

Introduce Blackline Master 9: Naming Parts

Objective: Identify the dependent clause and the conjunction of complex sentences.

Materials: Blackline Master 9; pencil

Form student pairs. Distribute Blackline Master 9. Read aloud the instructions together. Then have partners work together to write the dependent clause and the conjunction for each sentence.

Informal Assessment

Ask students to turn to page 8 in their textbooks. Ask a volunteer to create a complex sentence about the photos, using, for example, the conjunction *if. (If I go swimming, I might see a starfish.)* Then ask another student to repeat the conjunction and identify the dependent clause of the sentence.

Use the following chart to assess and reteach.

Are students able to: orally create complex sentences based on a visual?	Reteach using Guided Practice and illustrations on TE pages 8–9 for oral practice.
develop and demonstrate understanding of complex sentences?	Reteach using Language Support Activity on TE page 8.
complete complex sentences using context clues?	Reteach using the Reteach Activity on TE page 9.

Complex Conjunctions

```
Complex Conjunctions

unless      before      if
when        because     though
after       whenever    since
```

When You Find the Answer . . .

Look at each picture. Read each sentence. Complete each sentence with the best conjunction from the box.

after	before	unless	while

1. _____ José leaves the house, he grabs his book bag.

2. José studies _____ he is at school.

3. José goes over to Olivia's house _____ school gets out.

4. _____ it is raining, they always play outside.

Naming Parts

Look at the pictures. Read each sentence. On the line below, write the dependent clause. On the line below, write the conjunction.

1. Whenever my cousins visit, we go to the museum.

   Dependent Clause: _____

   Conjunction: _____

2. Before we go in, my father buys our tickets.

   Dependent Clause: _____

   Conjunction: _____

3. My cousin Cynthia looks at sculptures while I look at paintings.

   Dependent Clause: _____

   Conjunction: _____

4. We stay at the museum until it is time to go home.

   Dependent Clause: _____

   Conjunction: _____

COMBINING SENTENCES: COMPOUND SUBJECTS AND PREDICATES

I. DEVELOP ORAL LANGUAGE
Oral Focus on Grammar Skill

Objective: Orally convey understanding of compound subjects and compound predicates, and their structures.

Whole Group Oral Language Activity

Have the students look at the photograph on page 36. Write the word *Subject* on one side of the chalkboard. Ask: *Who is sitting by the campfire?* Write students' answers, such as, *A woman is sitting by the campfire,* under the heading. Then ask: *Who else is sitting by the fire?* Write that answer as well. *(A man is sitting by the campfire.)* Read the two sentences aloud. Have a volunteer point to the subject in both sentences. *(a woman; a man)* Now ask someone to say in one sentence what both people are doing. *(A woman and a man are sitting by the campfire.)* Write this sentence down and point out to students that these two sentences can be combined by joining the two subjects with the word *and.*

Now write the word *Predicate* on the other side of the chalkboard. Ask: *What is one thing the man on the right is doing?* Write students' answers, such as *The man is roasting marshmallows,* under this heading. Then ask: *What is one other thing the man is doing?* Write down this answer. *(The man is smiling.)* Next, have a volunteer say aloud the predicate in each sentence. Ask someone to say, in one sentence, two things the man is doing. *(The man is roasting marshmallows and smiling.)* Write this sentence on the chalkboard and explain that the word *and* also works here to combine two predicates into one compound sentence. Repeat the exercises using the conjunctions words *or* and *but.* Tell them that words that connect are called *conjunctions.*

Scaffolded Verbal Prompting
Use the following verbal prompts to help students better understand compound subjects and predicates.

Nonverbal Prompt for Active Participation

Pre-Production: *Point to one person in the picture. Show me what she is doing. Point to another person in the picture. Show me what he is doing. Now show me one thing both people are doing.*

One- or Two-Word Response Prompt

Early Production: *Name two people in the picture. Tell me one thing they are both doing.*

Prompt for Short Answers to Higher-Level Thinking Skills

Speech Emergence: *Tell me who is in the picture. Tell me two different things that person is doing.*

Prompt for Detailed Answers to Higher-Level Thinking Skills

Intermediate and Advanced Fluency: *Tell me, in one sentence, two things that one person in the picture is doing. Now tell me, in one sentence, one thing that two people are doing. Finally, tell me in one sentence, two choices one person in the picture could make.*

II. DEVELOP GRAMMAR SKILLS IN CONTEXT
Visual/Physical Focus on Grammar Skill

Objective: Use personal experiences to develop understanding of compound subjects and predicates.

Materials: Blackline Master 10, red, blue and yellow markers or crayons, scissors, craft sticks

Whole Group Activity

Invite students to sit in a large circle and tell about things they like to do. Provide each student with a copy of Blackline Master 10. Have them color each card, then cut them out. Tell them to paste the cards to sticks to make signs. Together, read aloud the words on each card: *and, but, or, compound subject, compound predicate.* Write a sentence, such as *I like to go hiking _____ camping.* Then read the sentence aloud and ask students to hold up the card with the conjunction that best fits. Invite volunteers to read aloud the completed compound sentence: *I like to go hiking and camping in the desert.* Review that *and* joins the two activities in one sentence. Have students hold up the card that best describes these two activities. *(Compound Predicate)* Repeat the exercise with student generated compound sentences that show contrasts *(but)* and choices *(or),* as well as compound subjects. *(My mom or dad will take me to the beach this weekend.)*

TPR

Extension: Write two or three of the sentences on the chalkboard. Ask volunteers to write CS next the compound subjects and CP next to the compound predicates.

Small Group Activity

Ask students to think about two things they will do this evening. *(I will do homework. I will eat dinner.)* Have volunteers act out these events. Invite other students to describe what they are doing. Remind students that the word *and* can join two activities that one person is doing to make one sentence. Have a student combine two sentences using *and* to make one compound predicate: *I will do homework and eat dinner.* Repeat the exercise using the conjunction *or.* *(I will do my math homework or my science homework first.)* Repeat the exercise focusing on compound subjects. *(My sister and I will play catch in the backyard; My brother or my sister will help me with my art project.)*

Partner Activity

Invite partners to use their cards from Blackline Master 10 to create and act out scenes about their interests. Model this by saying a simple sentence such as, *This summer I will fly to Florida.* Then pick a card and use it to make your simple sentence into a compound sentence with the conjunction and the compound card that have been picked. For instance: *This summer I will fly to Florida and visit my grandmother.* Invite each partner to act out his or her combined sentence.

Technology Link

Type pairs of simple sentences, having the same subject or predicate, on the computer. Invite pairs of varying language levels to work together to determine which conjunction would best make a compound sentence out of each pair of simple sentences. Have them delete and add the necessary punctuation and words. Ask each pair to read their new sentences aloud.

Use Blackline Masters 11 and 12 to help students create compound subjects and predicates.

Introduce Blackline Master 11: Puzzling and Piecing Together

Objective: Use context clues to create appropriate compounds.

Materials: Blackline Master 11; scissors

Explain to students that puzzle pieces are like parts of sentences: when you put them together, you have a whole picture. Putting parts of a sentence together makes a whole sentence. Divide the class into pairs of varying language levels. Guide students to cut out the puzzle pieces. Encourage pairs to read aloud each piece. Then have them move the pieces around until they have three sentences, each containing either a compound subject or a compound predicate. Finally, have students read aloud each combined sentence and identify the conjunctions.

Informal Assessment

Turn to page 19 in their textbooks. Read aloud a sentence from More Practice A. Ask: *Can you combine these sentences to contain a compound subject? How do you know?* Then turn to page 21 and repeat the exercise for compound predicates, using the first exercise from More Practice A.

Introduce Blackline Master 12: I like it, But . . .

Objective: To develop familiarity with conjunctions by completing compound sentences.

Materials: Blackline Master 12; pencils

Form student pairs. Distribute Blackline Master 12. Ask students to tell whether the first two sentences contain compound subjects or predicates. Read the directions aloud and discuss them with students. Ask partners to change the pairs of simple sentences into compound sentences, using *and, but,* or *or.*

Informal Assessment

Have students turn to page 19, and read aloud a pair of simple sentences from More Practice B. Ask: *How would you combine these two simple sentences to make a compound sentence?* Repeat the exercise on page 21 with compound predicates.

Use the following chart to assess and reteach.

Are students able to:	
orally describe a compound subject or predicate?	Reteach by practicing orally with using Guided Practice on TE pages 18 and 20.
combine two simple sentences to make a compound subject or predicate?	Reteach using Language Support Activity on TE pages 18 and 20.
determine the appropriate conjunction, using context clues?	Reteach using Reteach Activity on TE page 21.

Combining With Conjunctions

Color conjunctions red, the compound subject blue, and the compound predicate yellow. Cut out each heart and triangle. Glue each to a wood stick. Choose a card to display as different parts of a sentence are read.

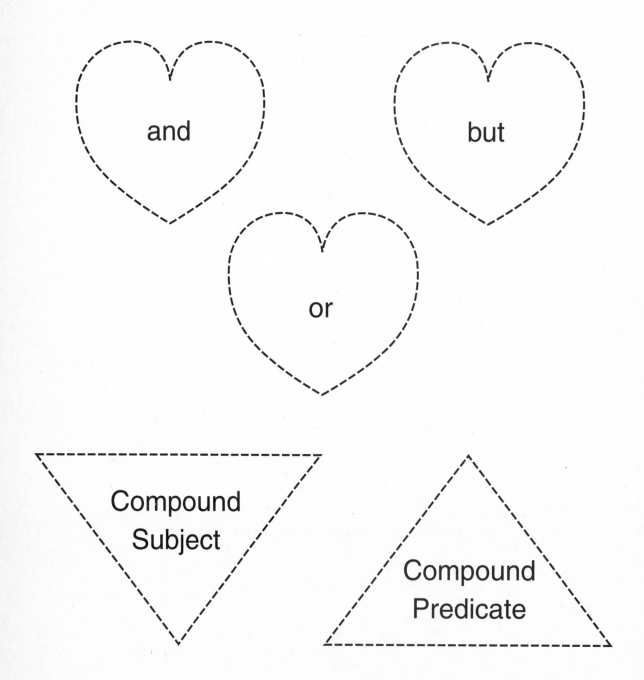

and

but

or

Compound
Subject

Compound
Predicate

Puzzling and Piecing Together

Cut out the puzzle pieces. Read each piece aloud. Move the pieces around until three compound sentences are formed. Read aloud each sentence and identify the compound subjects and predicates.

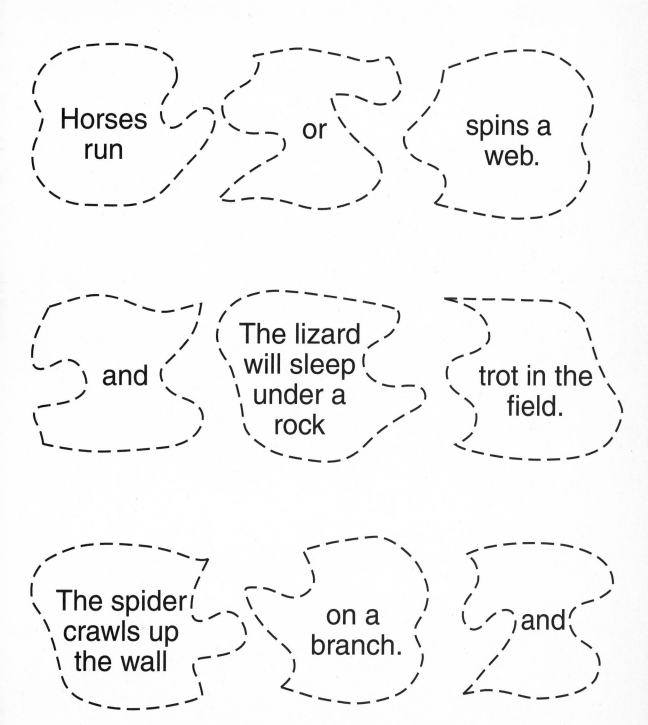

Horses run

or

spins a web.

and

The lizard will sleep under a rock

trot in the field.

The spider crawls up the wall

on a branch.

and

I Like It, But . . .

Look at the pictures. Read each pair of sentences. Combine the two sentences to make compound subjects or compound predicates. Write the new sentence on the line.

1. Jaime likes pancakes with syrup. Jaime likes pancakes with jam.

_____

2. My aunt Julie swims at the pool. I swim at the pool.

_____

3. Do you want to go to the park? Do you want to go to Ted's house?

_____

4. My uncle is from France. My aunt is from France.

_____

TIME-ORDER WORDS

Introduce this lesson before Pupil Edition pages 36–37.

I. DEVELOP ORAL LANGUAGE
Oral Focus on Vocabulary Skill

Objective: Orally connect his/her own experiences with those of others and describe the experience using time-order words.

Whole Group Oral Language Activity

Have five volunteers sit in a line of chairs labeled *first, second, third, next, last.* Have them tell a story about an adventure on a train or a bus. Explain to students that these words help tell the order in which a story or a trip happens. Have the first volunteer begin the story, starting his or her sentence with the word *first. (First, we stopped in Baltimore.)* Then invite the second volunteer to continue the story, beginning the sentence with the word *second.* Continue down the line until the story is finished. Then tape new words, such as *yesterday, today, as soon as, tomorrow,* and *finally,* to the seats. Invite a new set of volunteers to sit on the train or bus and tell a story.

Scaffolded Verbal Prompting

TPR

Use the following verbal prompts to help students better understand how time-order words might help a listener or reader understand when events happen, and in what order.

Nonverbal Prompt for Active Participation

Pre-Production: *Show me what happened on the trip first. Show me what happened on the trip second. Show me what happened on the trip last.*

One- or Two-Word Response Prompt

Early Production: *Say aloud three words that help tell what happened first, second, and third on the trip.*

Prompt for Short Answers to Higher-Level Thinking Skills

Speech Emergence: *Tell me what happened in the beginning. Tell me what happened next. Tell me what will happen in the end.*

Prompt for Detailed Answers to Higher-Level Thinking Skills

Intermediate and Advanced Fluency: *Tell me what happened on a trip you have taken. Tell me what happens each day. Which time-order words did you use to report about your adventure?*

II. DEVELOP VOCABULARY SKILLS IN CONTEXT
Visual/Physical Focus on Vocabulary Skill

Objective: Describe a place visually, using time-order words.

Small Group Activity

Have students work in small groups to present a "film" documentary about their neighborhoods. Invite students in each group to create a filmstrip out of large pieces of paper. Each student will work on at least one "frame." Explain that this film should show a tour of the students' neighborhoods and something they like about their neighborhoods. Encourage them to use time-order words, with pictures or sentences, to describe the order of events. Have students of varying language levels help one another write captions for the group's filmstrip.

Partner Activity

TPR

Write the following time-order words on the chalkboard: *first, today, now, before, after, tomorrow.* Tell pairs to play the part of someone who has never been to your school and someone who knows all about the school. Invite the first student to ask questions using the time-order words listed on the chalkboard. *(What do you do first when you come to school?)* Have the second student respond using the same time-order word. *(First, I hang up my coat.)* Have students act out their answers. When they have finished the whole list of time-words, have them switch roles and repeat the exercise.

Technology Link

Invite partners to type out their answers to the interviews in order to create a story in the correct time-order.

III. PRACTICE VOCABULARY SKILLS
Written Focus on Vocabulary Skill

Practice A

Objective: Identify time-order words and determine their correct placement

Materials: Blackline Master 13; scissors; paste

Introduce Blackline Master 13: Now You Add the Word!

Invite students to work in groups of three, giving each group a copy of Blackline Master 13. Read aloud the directions and each of the incomplete sentences. Have students cut out and paste the correct word from the word bank in the appropriate space. Then have students work together in their small groups to complete the remaining sentences.

Practice B

Objective: Develop knowledge of time-order words and use context clues to put events in order

Materials: Blackline Master 14; pencil; scissors

Introduce Blackline Master 14: Order on the Court!

Distribute Blackline Master 14. Read the paragraph aloud. Ask students to look at each of the four pictures and describe what is happening. Have pairs rearrange the pictures so that they appear in an order that makes the best sense. Then have them rewrite each paragraph, using time-order words so that the text and the pictures match. When students are finished, have each partner read the completed story aloud.

Informal Assessment

Ask students to turn to page 37 in the textbook. Have them look at the first exercise in Practice A. Ask, *Which words tell when the person started packing for the trip?* Then read aloud the sixth exercise in Practice B and ask, *Which word from the word bank would best fit here? Can you tell me why?*

Use the following chart to assess and reteach.

Are students able to: identify time-order words?	Reteach by using the Reteach Activity on TE page 37.
use context to know which time-order words are appropriate?	Reteach by using the Language Support Activity on TE page 36.

Now You Add the Word!

Look at the pictures. Read each sentence. Cut and paste the word that best fits each sentence.

_____ Bruce decided to visit his grandma.

_____ he asked his mother.

_____ Bruce got change for the bus.

_____ his brother packed some homemade cookies.

_____ Bruce was ready to go!

Word Bank

| Meanwhile | Next | First | Yesterday | Finally |

Order on the Court!

Read the paragraph. Look at the four pictures. Cut out the pictures and put them in the correct time-order. Write the time-order words in the paragraph that best completes each sentence.

_____ Sasha got to the court, she saw her friends. _____

they could play a game of basketball. _____ they had played for a

long time, everyone was happy and tired. "_____ we will play again!"

said Sasha.

After	As soon as	Tomorrow	Now

MAIN IDEA

Introduce this lesson before Pupil Edition pages 38–39.

I. DEVELOP ORAL LANGUAGE
Oral Focus on Composition Skill

Objective: To identify and develop understanding of main idea in a story by orally relating personal experiences

Whole Group Oral Language Activity

Direct students' attention to the photograph on page 39. Have students act out what they see. Ask: *Whom do you see? How do you think they know each other? What are they doing? What things in the picture help tell what is happening?* Write students' answers on the chalkboard. Ask the class for one idea that was common to all of their responses. Then ask: *Do you think this is the main idea of the photograph? Why? What images in the picture support your answer?*

TPR

Scaffolded Verbal Prompting

Use the following verbal prompts to help students better determine the main idea.

Nonverbal Prompt for Active Participation

Pre-Production: *Look at the picture. Show me what you would do if you were in the picture.*

One- or Two-Word Response Prompt

Early Production: *Tell me one important thing that is happening in the picture. Show me one thing you see in the picture that supports your answer.*

Prompt for Short Answers to Higher-Level Thinking Skills

Speech Emergence: *If you were going to write a caption below this picture, what would it say?*

Prompt for Detailed Answers to Higher-Level Thinking Skills

Intermediate Fluency: *How would you begin a story about the picture? What details would you include? What would you not include?*

II. DEVELOP COMPOSITION SKILLS IN CONTEXT
Visual/Physical Focus on Composition Skill

Objective: Develop understanding of main idea and supporting details through games.

Small Group Activity

Divide class into groups of five. Provide several pictures that are labeled with different main ideas, such as traveling in a car, taking care of a pet, and so on. Have one student pick a picture and act out the main idea. Tell other players to name the main idea. Whoever guesses the main idea gets one point. Players then each work to guess three supporting details that may be shown in the picture. Repeat until all group members have acted out a picture.

TPR

Technology Link

Have small groups work together to type out a list of supporting details for each picture whose main idea was identified.

Partner Activity

Extension: Ask partners to write a short paragraph about their illustrations, using the topic sentence to express the main idea and details to support it.

Have each student create a poster showing one activity he or she likes to do with friends or family. On the back, ask each partner to write the main idea of the poster as well as three supporting details that can be seen within the illustration. When finished, each partner should guess the main idea of the other's poster. To support the answer, have the partner point to and name three images that act as supporting details. When each partner has correctly named the main idea and supporting details, have them expand the main idea into a topic sentence that can be written at the top of each poster.

III. PRACTICE COMPOSITION SKILLS
Written Focus on Composition Skill

Practice A

Objective: Identify supporting details and a main idea

Materials: Blackline Master 15; scissors; crayons

Introduce Blackline Master 15: A Puzzling Picture

Hand out copies of Blackline Master 15. Review main idea and supporting details with students, reminding them that only important details should be used to support an idea. Invite partners to cut out the puzzle pieces and put the puzzle together using only the pieces that fit.

Practice B

Objective: Identify a topic sentence and supporting details

Determine placement of a topic sentence and supporting details using context clues.

Materials: Blackline Master 16; pencil

Introduce Blackline Master 16: Dear Pen Pal

Distribute copies of Blackline Master 16. Review main idea, topic sentences, and supporting details with students. Read aloud the letter and tell students that both the topic sentence and some supporting details are missing. Lead them to the box below the letter to look for sentences and phrases that will best complete the letter. When they have filled in the missing passages, ask students to label *TS* over the topic sentence and *SD* over each supporting detail.

Informal Assessment

Have students turn to page 39 in the textbook and look at Practice A. Read aloud the entire paragraph together. Then read the last sentence aloud to students and ask: *Is this the topic sentence? Why or why not? Is it a supporting detail? Why or why not?*

Use the following chart to assess and reteach.

Are students able to: identify and develop understanding of the main idea in a story?	Reteach by using the Language Support Activity on TE page 38.
develop understanding of main idea and supporting details through games?	Reteach by using the Reteach Activity on TE page 39.

A Puzzling Picture

Cut out the puzzle pieces. Read each puzzle piece carefully. Choose which pieces support the main idea. Put only the pieces that work as supporting details together to create the whole picture.

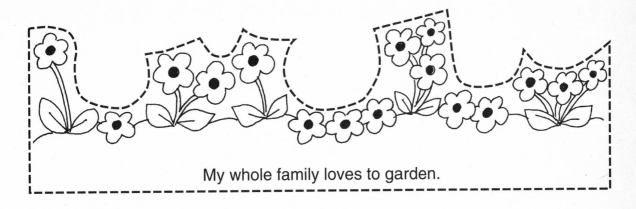

My whole family loves to garden.

Dad does the weeding.

Joe is ready to play.

Mom and Joe water the garden.

I plant the seeds for the new flowers.

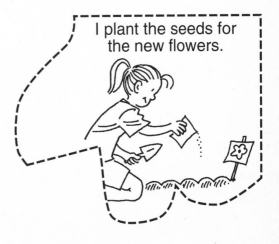

Dear Pen Pal

Read the letter aloud. Read the phrases from the word bank. Choose which phrase would best work as the main idea and supporting details of the letter and write them in. Label the main idea "MI" and the supporting details "SD".

Dear Pen Pal,

(1) _____. I had wanted to visit ever since I

started writing you. (2) _____. All your other

animals were fun, too. The first morning, it seemed like your

rooster woke me up too early. (3) _____.

They made me laugh when they squealed. I also had a lot of

fun playing in your barn. (4) _____. Next

time, maybe you can show me how to milk the cows!

Sincerely,
Your Pen Pal

1. Staying home is a lot of fun.	I had a great time visiting you on your farm.
2. First of all, I loved riding your horses.	First of all, I love riding sailboats.
3. But then it was fun to feed the pigs.	But then it was fun to go shopping.
4. The hayloft is better than a playground!	The hayloft was empty.

Introduce this lesson before Pupil Edition pages 44–63.

I. PREWRITE
Oral Warm Up

Objectives:
• Determine the purpose for listening, such as to gain information
• Relate observations, or recollections about an experience

Whole Group Oral Language Activity

Write the word *State* on the chalkboard. Invite a volunteer to come up to a map of the United States and point to the state in which the people in your school reside. Write the name of that state under the heading. Then ask other volunteers to come to the map and point to and name different states they have visited.

Have volunteers ask questions about the listed states. For instance, a student may ask: *What is Louisiana like in the wintertime? What did you do when you went there? Where did you stay? Do you want to go back? Why or why not?* Ask students who have an association with that state to answer each question. Write the responses next to the appropriate state name.

Graphic Organizer

Objectives: Think about the audience and purpose of the personal narrative during prewrite.

Use a graphic organizer to record experiences.

Materials: Blackline Master 17; pencils

Introduce the Writing Mode

Explain to students that a personal narrative is a piece of writing that tells about an experience they have had and how they feel about it. Use the list to create a personal narrative from the information gathered there. (*Last August I visited New Mexico with my family. At first it was strange, because it was so different from home. Then I noticed ravens and coyotes and wild rabbits. I got to see how big the sky looks in the desert. Sometimes it seemed like the moon was close enough to touch! I hope I get to go back there next summer.*) Have volunteers create other sentences that tell of a personal experience about states in this country.

Pre-Production and Early Production

Scaffolded Writing Instruction

Distribute copies of Blackline Master 17. Invite students to draw pictures in the top box and in the following boxes.

Speech Emergence

Invite students to label their pictures with words or phrases. Ask them to use the labeled pictures to help them describe what they did and how they felt.

Intermediate and Advanced Fluency

Ask students to use the words they wrote in the chart to create sentences about their personal narratives.

Individual Activity

Research and Inquiry

Model using the dictionary by looking up an unfamiliar word from the personal experiences students have drawn in Blackline Master 17. For instance, look up the word *capital*, checking its spelling, meanings, and part of speech. Encourage students to refer to the dictionary while finishing Blackline Master 17.

II. DRAFT
Focus on Personal Narrative

Objectives:
- Organize ideas using sequencing strategies
- Begin to draft a personal narrative

Model the process of choosing a main idea for a personal narrative. Write the main idea and some supporting details for a personal narrative on the chalkboard: *Last week my Mom and I picked up my oldest brother at the airport. He was coming from Hawaii, where he works. At the airport I was the first to see him. I ran up and gave him a big hug.* Read the sentences aloud, then ask students to choose which sentence best represents the main idea of the story. Ask a volunteer to write the initials *MI* for main idea above the appropriate sentence. Have another volunteer write the initials *SD* above the sentences that function as supporting details. Then ask one student to read aloud the story while others act it out.

Scaffolded Writing Instruction

TPR

Pre-Production and Early Production

Blackline Master 18: I Support That Idea

Use Blackline Master 18 to help students develop the main idea and supporting details of their personal narratives. Have them draw or use pictures from magazines to show the main idea and supporting details of their story. Encourage them to use as much detail as possible in their illustrations.

Speech Emergence

Blackline Master 19: First, Have an Idea

Have students use Blackline Master 19 to assist them in writing their personal narratives. Remind them to use sentences that connect to each other, using time-order words where necessary.

Intermediate and Advanced Fluency

Invite students to begin composing their personal narratives. Before they write, review the features of a personal narrative with them, and encourage them to use these elements. Remind students that time-order words work well to connect ideas in a clear order.

III. REVISE
Focus on Word Choice

Objectives:
- Revise a personal narrative
- Elaborate details

Write the following paragraph on the chalkboard and read it aloud with the class:

Yesterday, I had a great time with my dog Amy. We played catch in the backyard. Then we walked to the park with my mom. After a short nap by the lake, we had a picnic. We went home and I brushed Amy's hair.

TPR

Invite students to suggest how the sequence of the story could be made more clear by adding time-order words. Prompt students with questions such as the following: *When did they play in the backyard?* (possible answers: First; in the morning) *What word would help show that going home and brushing the dog's hair was the last thing that happened?* (finally)

Scaffolded Instruction for Revising

Pre-Production and Early Production
Blackline Master 18: I Support That Idea

Speech Emergence
Blackline Master 19: First, Have an Idea

Intermediate and Advanced Fluency

Have students refer to Blackline Master 18 to help them understand time-order words. Ask them how they could show when something is happening in their pictures, to make the sequence of the story clear.

Ask students to return to Blackline Master 19 and add words to their personal narratives that will help the reader understand more clearly the sequence of events.

Have students review their personal narratives and use a dictionary or thesaurus to choose time-order words that will clarify the sequence of events.

Technology Link

Invite partners to type their personal narratives into a computer. Then ask them to use the insert function to add time-order words to their narrative.

IV. REVISE • PEER CONFERENCING
Focus on Peer Conferencing

Objectives:
- Participate in peer conferences
- Offer and receive constructive feedback and suggestions for improvement
- Revise voice and flow of personal narrative

Paired Activity

Have pre-production and early-production students work in pairs with more advanced students to hold peer conferences. Encourage the advanced fluency students to share what they see in the illustrations created by the pre- and early-production students. Encourage them to help provide English vocabulary words to add to the personal narrative.

Turn to page 57 and use the checklist as a model. On the chalkboard, write a similar checklist for each proficiency level and invite students to use this as they hold their peer conferences.

V. PROOFREADING
Focus on English Conventions

Objectives:
- Proofread narratives for grammatical and other errors
- Use complex sentences

Say these dependent clauses and ask why they are not complete sentences. *Before I learned how to swim. Wherever I go on vacation.*

Review that dependent clauses cannot stand alone because they begin with conjunctions. Ask students what is missing in both lines. (an independent clause) Have a volunteer add an independent clause to the first line. (Possible answer: *Before I learned to swim, I was afraid to go near the water.*) Tell students that looking carefully at what has been written and correcting any errors, as they have just done, is called proofreading.

[Answers for Blackline Master 20

Part A:
1. DC   IC
2. IC   DC
3. DC   IC

Part B:
4. Since it was hot, I decided to stop for a drink.
5. After I got home I put my bike in the garage.
6. Since I didn't have a quarter, he let me pay with two marbles.
7. While I was riding my bike, I saw a friend selling lemonade.

Part C: Answers will vary.]

Have students complete Blackline Master 20 for extra practice on the grammar skill before they review their writing for any possible misuse of dependent clauses.

When students have completed Blackline Master 20, explain that proofreading also includes correcting spelling mistakes. As several students may have difficulty with the same words, you might wish to create an open-ended spelling book for the class to use. Each time a new word needs to be entered, have a student work with you on spelling the word out before you write it into the book.

Model using the dictionary by looking up a word suggested by a volunteer. Ask the volunteer what letter the word starts with and turn to the first page of that section. Then ask what the second letter may be, and so on, until you find the correct spelling of the word.

VI. PUBLISH

Objective: Present personal narratives to an audience

Spelling Tip: Have students keep a list of homophones, such as *there, their*, and *they're*, and the definitions of each. When a student questions which spelling is correct for a particular meaning, they can refer to their list.

TPR

Turn to the checklist on page 60 and use it as a model for preparing a checklist for each proficiency level. Write your checklist on the chalkboard and have students refer to it as they prepare the final version of their personal narrative.

Create Bookstore Corners

Have students work in small groups to create "bookstores" for each of their personal narratives. Invite each group to present to the rest of the class the "books" in their bookstores. Have fluent students read aloud their narratives, and invite students who drew their personal narratives to display each illustration sequentially to tell their story.

VII. LISTENING, SPEAKING, VIEWING, REPRESENTING

Refer to the steps on pages 62–63 as models for creating activities that will encourage students of all language levels to share their talents and ideas with the rest of the class. Encourage students at pre- or early-production levels to participate by acting out or helping to illustrate their own or other students' personal narratives.

TPR

Informal Assessment

As you assess students' writing and learning development, you will need to adapt your expectations about the appropriateness of each student's response. For instance, rather than expect a student to provide an oral response to a writing prompt, you might encourage students to express their answers through physical activities that show their understanding of a concept.

Story Chart

Choose a state you talked about with your class. Draw a picture that represents that state in the top box. In the left-hand boxes, draw and write what you have done there. In the right-hand boxes draw and write how each activity made you feel.

Place

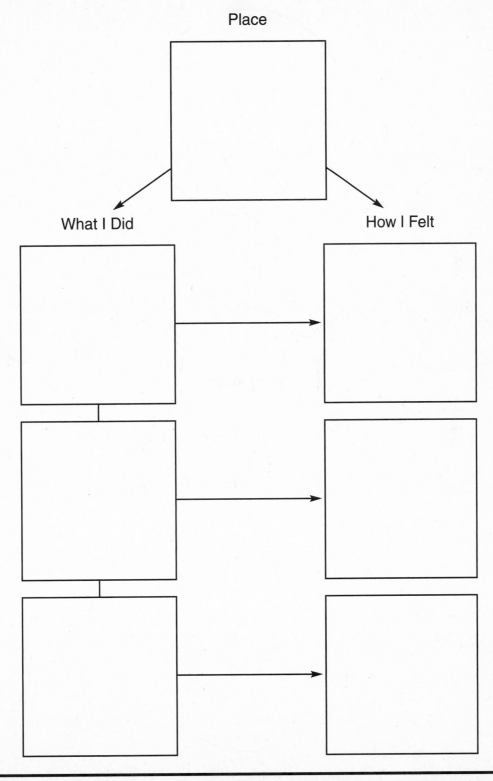

What I Did

How I Felt

I Support That Idea

Think about the main idea of your state story. In the center circle, draw or write your main idea. In the surrounding circles, draw or write supporting details.

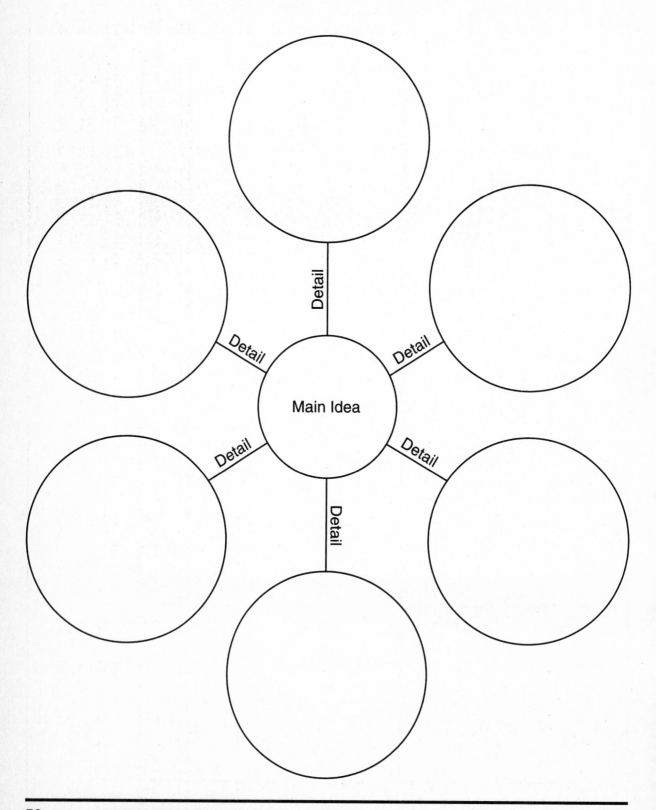

First, Get an Idea

Think about your experience. Use sentences with time-order words to tell your story. Illustrate the sequence of the story with detailed pictures.

I remember when _____. First, _____. Next,

_____. Then, _____. After that

_____. Finally, _____.

Complex Sentences

A. Write the initials *DC* above each dependent clause and *IC* above each independent clause in the following sentences.

1. Whenever I ride my bike, I wear a helmet.

2. I make sure my tires are full before I go out.

3. Although my street is quiet, I always look for traffic.

B. Combine the dependent clauses and independent clauses below.

4. Because it was hot.
   I decided to stop for a drink.

   _____

5. After I got home.
   I put my bike in the garage.

   _____

6. Since I didn't have a quarter.
   He let me pay with two marbles.

   _____

7. While I was riding my bike.
   I saw a friend selling lemonade.

   _____

C. Rewrite the sentences from Exercise B in a logical sequence.

Dear Journal,

_____

_____

_____

_____

_____

SINGULAR AND PLURAL NOUNS

I. DEVELOP ORAL LANGUAGE
Oral Focus on Grammar Skill

Objective: Orally clarify and support spoken ideas with evidence, elaborations, and examples of singular and plural nouns.

TPR

Whole Group Oral Language Activity

Write the words *People, Places, Things, Ideas* on the chalkboard. Ask students to look at the photographs on pages 140–141. Ask: *Point to a person on the page.* Continue with other examples: *Point to a place on the page. Point to a thing on the page.* Have volunteers name each person, place, and thing. Have others act out or name one picture they see. Write each student's response under the correct heading. Also discuss ideas, such as *peace* or *freedom.*

Tell the class that each of these words is a *singular noun.* Select a category from those listed on the board. Have students page through the unit to find two or more pictures of a noun to list in that category. Tell students that nouns that name more than one person, place, thing, or idea are *plural nouns.* Most plural nouns add *-s* or *-es.* For an example, use the pictures on pages 86 and 87. Ask: *Who are those people? How many are there? Count them.* List the plural noun *girls* under *People.* Have volunteers find examples for each category. Have others act out or name other nouns they see. As nouns are added to each category, list the singular and plural form for each word. Brainstorm the ways in which certain nouns are alike and the ways in which they are different.

Scaffolded Verbal Prompting

Use the following verbal prompts to help students better understand singular and plural nouns.

Nonverbal Prompt for Active Participation

Pre-Production: *Look at the picture. Point to a person (place, thing). Point to two people. Point to a picture that shows two or more objects.*

One- or Two-Word Response Prompt

Early Production: *Who is in the picture? Tell me how many people (places, things) you can see.*

Prompt for Short Answers to Higher-Level Thinking Skills

Speech Emergence: *Pick three pictures with people. Tell me the page numbers and who you see. Pick two pictures with things. Tell me the page numbers and what you see. Find pictures of two places. Can you tell me something about what you see?*

Prompt for Detailed Answers to Higher-Level Thinking Skills

Intermediate and Advanced Fluency: *Select two pictures. Tell me in one or two sentences, who or what is in each picture. How can you tell if a noun is singular? What were some of the plural nouns you named?*

II. DEVELOP GRAMMAR SKILLS IN CONTEXT
Visual/Physical Focus on Grammar Skill

Objective: Develop and demonstrate understanding of singular and plural nouns.

Materials: Blackline Master 21, pencils

TPR

Extension: Students can each draw two pictures of interesting things that they do. (Examples: *sports, hobbies, activities.*). Challenge them to draw one picture of something that they like to do alone and another showing what they like to do with their family. After exchanging their drawing with a partner, have the partner name the singular and plural nouns of people, places, things, or ideas in the pictures.

Whole Group Activity

Provide each student with a copy of Blackline Master 21. Instruct students to use pencils to complete their drawing. Then invite volunteers to describe and compare their families aloud. Have the students answer the questions on the blackline master. Invite students to share their answers to the questions. Ask students to identify the words that name more than one family member. Write those on the chalkboard. (Examples: *brothers, sisters, cousins.*) Point out the final -*s* in each plural noun.

Small Group Activity

Ask groups to assign themselves roles of family members. Have them pantomime an activity they do together as a family. Be sensitive to student's feelings about discussing families, but challenge them to make the family situations realistic. After the groups complete their skits, ask students to name and number the family members in each group. (Examples: *one parent, two brothers, three sisters.*) Discuss what is similar and different about each family.

Partner Activity

Invite students to work with a partner. Have them ask each other the questions on Blackline Master 21. Then have them show their pictures to their partners and describe their families. Ask them to act out one thing that they like to do with their family

Technology Link

Type sentences that contain errors involving singular and plural nouns into the computer.

Two girl wanted to ride their bikes to a parks.

Many cloud are in the sky and the weathers is cold.

Include context clues in the sentences to indicate if a noun should be singular or plural. Pair students of varying language levels to proofread the sentences and edit nouns so the correct singular or plural forms are used.

III. PRACTICE GRAMMAR SKILLS
Written Focus on Grammar Skill

Use Blackline Masters 22 and 23 to reinforce students' knowledge of singular and plural nouns.

Introduce Blackline Master 22: One, or More Than One?

Objective: Identify singular and plural nouns.

Materials: Blackline Master 22; scissors

[**Answers**—singular nouns: baby, student; plural nouns: teachers, turkeys, foxes, bushes, friends, inches, lifeguards]

Distribute Blackline Master 22. Read aloud and discuss the directions with students. Model the first example. After the students complete their work, have volunteers share their answers. Then have students cut out the boxes on the blackline master to make word/picture cards. Have students take turns showing each other the cards and having them say the singular or plural version of the item(s) pictured.

Informal Assessment

Direct students to the pictures on pages 92 and 93. Have students identify what they see. Ask, *Did you name a singular or a plural noun?* For plural nouns, ask, *How does the word change to show the plural form?* Repeat with other examples.

Introduce Blackline Master 23: Singular or Plural?

Objective: Choose the correct singular or plural form of a noun.

Materials: Blackline Master 23; pencils

[**Answers:** 1. reunions; 2. races, games; 3. family; 4. baby, party; 5. race; 6. stories]

Distribute Blackline Master 23. Discuss the illustration. Write the headings on the board: *Singular* and *Plural.* Ask students to name all the singular nouns that they see in the picture. Then have them name all the plural nouns. Write the responses under the correct headings. Read aloud and discuss activity directions with students. Read aloud each sentence or have volunteers read them aloud. Complete the first example together. Have students work individually to complete the rest of the sentences.

Informal Assessment

Have students turn to page 135 and identify the people, places, and things that they see in the picture. Say: *Name words that are singular. Name other words that are plural. How might you use those words in a sentence?*

Use the following chart to assess and reteach.

Are students able to:	
orally identify people, places, things, and ideas in a picture?	Reteach using the Language Support Activity on TE page 86 for oral practice.
put singular and plural nouns into sentences?	Reteach using the Language Support Activity on TE page 88.
identify the singular and plural forms of nouns?	Reteach using the Reteach Activity on TE page 89.

My Family

Draw a picture of your family. With a partner, answer the questions.

1. How many people are in your family? _____

2. Do you have any brothers and sisters? _____

3. How many brothers and sisters do you have? _____

4. Name one thing you like to do together. _____

One, or More Than One?

Look at the pictures. Read the word below the pictures. Underline the picture of a singular noun. Circle the picture of a plural noun and write its plural form beside the word.

teacher _____

baby _____

turkey _____

fox _____

student _____

bush _____

friend _____

inch _____

lifeguard _____

Singular or Plural?

Look at the picture. Read each sentence. Circle the word that correctly completes each sentence. Write the word or words on the line.

1. Family reunion/reunions at the lake are fun. _____

2. There are race/races and game/games, too. _____ _____

3. My family/families went to the reunion. _____

4. The new baby/babies was happy at the party/parties.

   _____ _____

5. The children ran a race/races across the grass. _____

6. My grandfather told us many story/stories. _____

I. DEVELOP ORAL LANGUAGE
Oral Focus on Grammar Skill

Objective: Orally describe pictures using singular and plural nouns, particularly the forms of irregular plurals.

Whole Group Oral Language Activity

Ask students to look at the photographs on pages 122 and 123. Ask, *What is alike and what is different in each photograph? Point to one boy/girl on the page. Count the number of boys/girls. Point to one child on the page. Count the number of children.* Sum up their responses: *One boy. Three boys. One child. Six children.* Write some of the singular nouns and their plurals on the board. Ask, *What sounds form the plural of each word?* Show students that not all words form the plural by just adding *-s,* or *-es.*

Write these words on the board, but cover the plural form with a piece of paper.

man	*men*
woman	*women*
tooth	*teeth*

Ask volunteers to say the plural form of each word. Remove the paper and verify the answer. Have the students choral read the singular and plural forms. Continue with other examples from the student edition, pages 88–89. (Examples: *leaf/leaves; piano/pianos; deer/deer; potato/potatoes*). Explain common rules such as *f, fe = ves, y = ies.*

Scaffolded Verbal Prompting

Use the following verbal prompts to help students better understand irregular plural nouns.

Nonverbal Prompt for Active Participation

Pre-Production: *Look at the picture. Listen to the words. Raise one finger for a singular noun, two fingers for a plural noun.* (Examples: *man/men; woman/women; child/children*)

One- or Two-Word Response Prompt

Early Production: *Who is in the picture? Tell me how many men/women you can see.*

Prompt for Short Answers to Higher-Level Thinking Skills

Speech Emergence: *Tell me how many children are in the pictures. How many men? How many women? Which words did you use to describe more than one person?*

Prompt for Detailed Answers to Higher-Level Thinking Skills

Intermediate and Advanced Fluency: *Tell me, in one sentence, who or what is in the pictures. What words did you use to identify singular nouns? What words did you use to name plural nouns?*

II. DEVELOP GRAMMAR SKILLS IN CONTEXT
Visual/Physical Focus on Grammar Skill

Objective: Develop and demonstrate understanding of how to form irregular plural nouns.

Materials: Blackline Master 24, crayons

TPR

TPR

Extension: Challenge students to sort the word cards according to the rules followed for forming plurals. (Examples: words that end in *f, fe;* words that end in *o;* same form for singular and plural.) Then they may re-sort the word cards according to whether the nouns name people, places, or things.

Whole Group Activity

Provide each student with a copy of Blackline Master 24. Instruct students to use crayons to color the top card red, the middle card green, and the bottom card yellow. Have students cut out each card. Tell students to hold up the red card when they hear a singular noun, a green card when they hear a plural noun, and a yellow card when the word can be singular or plural. Model this procedure with the words, *leaves, leaf; moose, moose.* Repeat with other singular and plural nouns. Encourage volunteers to use the words in a sentence.

Small Group Activity

Have students work in two groups. Assign one group to act out a visit to the farm, while the other group will act out a visit to the city. Have them describe and pantomime the people, animals, and things that they see. Encourage them to include as many irregular plurals as they can. (Examples: *men, women, tomatoes, mice*) After each group has performed, use a Venn diagram to show what things are the same and what things are different on the farm and in the city. Use the nouns on the diagram to make singular or plural forms.

Partner Activity

Make a deck of singular and plural word cards for each pair of students. One set should only name singular nouns and the other set should name their plurals. Have students shuffle their cards together. Have partners match the singular and plural word cards.

Technology Link

Type a list of singular and plural nouns into a word processing program. Type each plural noun as if it ended in *-s.* Have students use the computer to spell-check the list and correct the misspelled plurals. Ask students to read aloud the correct pairs of words. Then have them write the words in sentences and use the spell-check to proof their work.

III. PRACTICE GRAMMAR SKILLS
Written Focus on Grammar Skill

Use Blackline Masters 25 and 26 to reinforce the use of irregular singular and plural nouns.

Introduce Blackline Master 25: Match Them Up!

Objective: Identify irregular singular and plural nouns.

Materials: Blackline Master 25

Distribute Blackline Master 25. Read aloud and discuss the directions with students. After the students complete their work, have volunteers share their answers. Have students cut out the framed pictures on the blackline master to make picture cards. Have students take turns showing each other the cards and naming the plural form of the word.

Informal Assessment

Give each student six index cards. Choose one word from each rule listed on page 88. Ask students to find each word in a dictionary and write its plural form on a separate card. Have volunteers identify the letters that changed to make each plural form. As they do this, review the rules for changing the words from singular to plural.

Introduce Blackline Master 26: Find It

Objective: Demonstrate knowledge of irregular plural nouns.

Materials: Blackline Master 26; pencils

Distribute Blackline Master 26. Have students identify each picture. Read aloud and discuss activity directions with students. Model the first example. Have students work independently or in pairs to complete the rest of the exercise. After students have completed their work, ask them to provide the singular and the plural form of each picture and use the words in a sentence.

Informal Assessment

Write these sentences on the chalkboard:

1. Some deer and one moose wandered through the forest.

2. These animal videos are available to rent.

3. A few women, but only one man, worked on the farm.

Ask: *Which nouns are singular? Name the nouns that are plural. Which words name people? places? things?*

Use the following chart to assess and reteach.

Are students able to:	
orally identify irregular singular and plural nouns?	Reteach using the Language Support Activity on TE page 88.
change singular nouns to the irregular plural form?	Reteach using the Language Support Activity on TE page 86.
identify irregular plural nouns and their singular form?	Reteach using the Reteach Activity on TE page 89.

Identify the Nouns

Use crayons to color the top card red, the middle card green, and the bottom card yellow. Cut out each card. Hold up the red card when you hear a singular noun, a green card when you hear a plural noun, and a yellow card when the noun form is singular or plural.

Singular

Plural

Singular or Plural

Match Them Up!

Look at each picture and singular noun. Read each plural noun. Match the picture to its plural form.

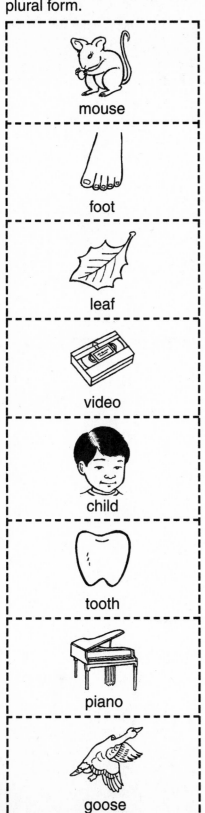

- leaves

- children

- mice

- feet

- teeth

- videos

- geese

- pianos

Find It

Look at each picture. Say and write the plural form of the noun in the picture. Find and circle the plural forms of the nouns in the puzzle.

_____ _____ _____ _____ _____

_____ _____ _____ _____ _____

h	r	h	a	l	v	e	s	p
t	o	d	j	m	i	c	e	t
e	h	w	i	q	d	e	e	r
e	m	o	o	s	e	t	y	o
t	o	m	a	t	o	e	s	u
m	x	e	k	e	s	u	w	t
r	v	n	t	e	e	t	h	y
c	h	i	l	d	r	e	n	m

I. DEVELOP ORAL LANGUAGE
Oral Focus on Grammar Skill

Objective: Orally describe and distinguish common and proper nouns.

Whole Group Oral Language Activity

Display a world map and a collection of pictures of famous people collected from magazines. Begin by talking about what you would do if you could spend time with a famous person anywhere in the world. Specify the name of the person and the place. Point out the place on the map. (Example: *I would like to spend time with Cesar Chavez in California.*) Ask students to choose a person and a place. Ask: *Show me a picture of the person or name him (or her). Find that place on the map.* Remind students to provide specific names and places. Write them on the board. Discuss what is alike or different about these people and places.

Help students understand the difference between common and proper nouns. Review common nouns. Remind students that nouns name people, places, things, and ideas. Tell students that a proper noun names a particular person, place, or thing. Write the words *Person, Place,* and *Thing* across the board. Have students refer to the maps and pictures that you have displayed to provide particular examples of common nouns in each category. Brainstorm proper nouns for each of these categories. Tell students they may include brand names for products. Record their answers under the correct heading.

Scaffolded Verbal Prompting

Use the following verbal prompts to help students better understand common and proper nouns.

Nonverbal Prompt for Active Participation

Pre-Production: *Look at the pictures. Point to a person. Point to (name a well-known individual in one of the photos). Look at the map. Show me where you were born.*

One- or Two-Word Response Prompt

Early Production: *Name a person in one of the pictures. Tell me something that you might say to that person. Point to a country on the map. What is the name of the country?*

Prompt for Short Answers to Higher-Level Thinking Skills

Speech Emergence: *Tell me who is in the picture. What would you like to do with that person? What would you like to ask that person? Where would you like to meet that person?*

Prompt for Detailed Answers to Higher-Level Thinking Skills

Intermediate and Advanced Fluency: *Tell me whom you would like to meet. Where would you like to meet that person? Say the sentence once more. Which words in the sentence are common nouns? Which words are proper nouns?*

II. DEVELOP GRAMMAR SKILLS IN CONTEXT
Visual/Physical Focus on Grammar Skill

Objective: Develop and demonstrate understanding of common and proper nouns.

Materials: Blackline Master 27; newspapers; scissors; magazines; index cards; paste; social studies, reading, or history textbooks

TPR

Whole Group Activity

Write a list of common nouns, such as *teacher, movie star, basketball player, book, computer game, clothing,* on the chalkboard. Read them aloud and tell students that these words are common nouns because they name general people, places, and things. Distribute newspapers and magazines. Give students some time to find examples of common nouns. Then have volunteers brainstorm proper nouns as examples of the common nouns that they found. Remind students that proper nouns name particular people, places, or things and that they always begin with a capital letter. List the students' responses. Use TPR commands to categorize the words on the list. (Examples: *Go to the board. Underline a proper noun that names a person (place, thing). Circle the initial capital letter.*) Continue with other examples. Challenge students to discuss the nouns in each category in terms of which common nouns are alike and which ones are different. (Examples: *Which nouns name women? Which nouns name men? Which places are in the United States? Which places are in other countries?*)

TPR

Small Group Activity

Provide each group with a copy of Blackline Master 27 and a stack of index cards. Have students cut out the letters and paste one on each card. Assign different passages from a history, social studies, or reading textbook. Challenge students to find a proper noun that starts with each letter of the alphabet. Have them write it on the appropriate index card. Have students share their work. Encourage them to use the cards to learn and review the proper nouns.

Extension: Students may be asked to provide proper noun examples on the back of the pages of their common noun alphabet book. Examples:

Lake Superior is a lake. It is one of the Great Lakes.
Mount St. Helens is an active volcano.
Mr. Johnson is our computer teacher.

Partner Activity

Place the alphabet letters from Blackline Master 27 in a bag. Have each group select five or six letters. Have the partners go on a scavenger hunt for newspaper and magazine pictures of common nouns that begin with that letter. Have them paste each picture on drawing paper and label it. Illustrate the word if necessary. Combine the pages to make a common noun alphabet book.

Technology Link

Type Activity B from More Practice on page 91 into a word processing program. Pair students of varying language levels. Have students spell check the activity. Ask students to list the common nouns and proper nouns in each sentence. Point out any differences between what is provided in the spell-check program and what is actually correct. (*Oak Street, Library.*)

III. PRACTICE GRAMMAR SKILLS
Written Focus on Grammar Skill

Use Blackline Masters 28 and 29 to reinforce the concept of common and proper nouns.

Introduce Blackline Master 28: Mapping Common and Proper Places

Objective: Identify common and proper nouns in context.

Materials: Blackline Master 28; wall map of the U.S., scissors, glue or paste

Distribute Blackline Master 28. Read aloud and discuss the directions with students. Divide the class into pairs of varying language proficiencies to complete the activity. Guide students to cut out the label pieces. Refer students to the classroom map. Then have students paste the labels on the map. Add additional proper nouns. (Examples: your own state, city, landmarks.)

Informal Assessment

Have students look at the Blackline Master 28. Read aloud a common or proper noun. Ask, *Point to the word on the map. Is this a common noun or a proper noun? What letters are clues to indicate what kind of noun it is?* Repeat the questioning with other examples.

Introduce Blackline Master 29: Common and Proper Places

Objective: Distinguish between common and proper nouns and use them correctly.

Materials: Blackline Master 29; pencils

[Answers: Part A: mountain-Mt. Everest, country-United States, lake-Lake Michigan, city-New York City, capital-Washington, D.C.; **Part B:** 1. proper, 2. common, 3. proper, 4. common, 5. proper]

Form student pairs. Distribute Blackline Master 29. Read aloud and discuss activity directions with students. Look at **Part A.** Identify the illustrations under Proper Nouns. Complete the first example together. Look at **Part B.** Complete the first example together. Ask the students to work in pairs to complete the rest of the exercises.

Informal Assessment

Have students turn to page 90 and point to the photo on the page. Ask, *What do you see here? What is a common noun that names or tells about this place? What country do you think this is in? Is the name of the country a common or proper noun? Can you use both the common noun and the proper noun in a sentence?*

Use the following chart to assess and reteach.

Are students able to:	
orally identify common and proper nouns?	Reteach using the Language Support Activity on TE page 90 for oral practice.
identify common and proper nouns in context?	Reteach using the Language Support Activity on TE page 92.
distinguish between common and proper nouns in a sentence?	Reteach using the Reteach Activity on TE page 93.

Alphabetical Order

Read the letter on each block. Cut out the letters and mix them up. Then put them back in alphabetical order.

A	B	C	D	E
F	G	H	I	J
K	L	M	N	O
P	Q	R	S	T
U	V	W	X	Y
Z				

Mapping Common and Proper Places

Cut out each label. Match the label to where it belongs on the map and paste it down. Underline the common nouns. Circle the proper nouns.

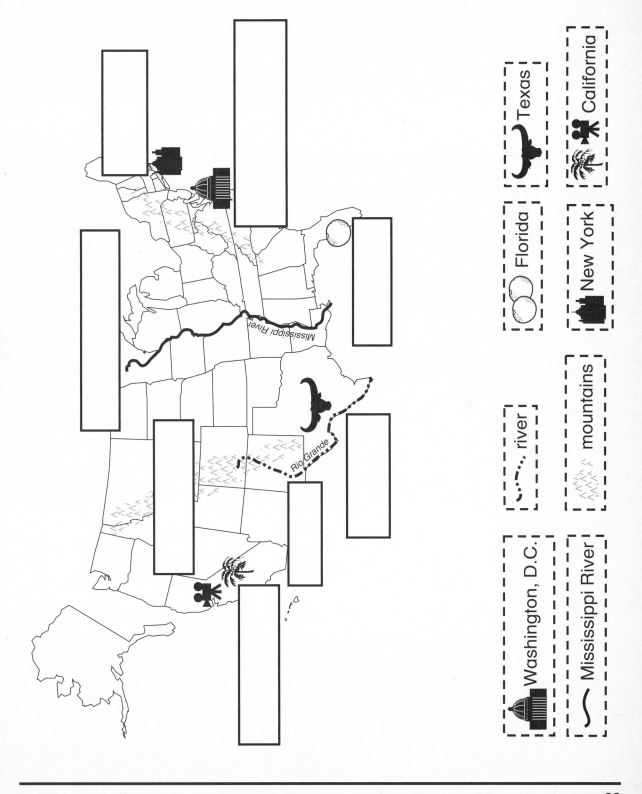

Common and Proper Places

Part A.

Read the common nouns. Look at the pictures. Match the common nouns to the proper nouns.

Common Nouns   **Proper Nouns**

mountain   Lake Michigan

country   Mt. Everest

lake   United States

city   New York City

capital   Washington, D.C.

Part B.

Read each sentence. Write *common* or *proper* to describe each underlined noun.

1. Many boats travel on the <u>Mississippi River</u>. _____

2. People from many <u>countries</u> come to the United States. _____

3. Teresa studies at the <u>Denver Library</u>. _____

4. The <u>students</u> finished their reports by Friday. _____

5. Our class is comparing the animals of <u>Africa</u> and Australia. _____

I. DEVELOP ORAL LANGUAGE
Oral Focus on Grammar Skill

Objective: Orally apply knowledge of letter-sound correspondences, language structure, and context to recognize possessive nouns.

Whole Group Oral Language Activity

Invite students to display four or five items from their desks, lockers, or knapsacks. At random, choose an item. Ask, *Whose (item) is this?* Have a volunteer provide the possessive form and verify the response. (Example: *This is Juan's pencil.*) Continue selecting new students and different items, as you have students repeat the first sentence and add another sentence using the possessive form. (Example: *This is Juan's pencil. This is Sylvie's notebook.*) Then write the examples on the board. Try to include words that already end with *-s.* Begin the go-around again until all the students have had a turn.

Guide students through the explanation of possessive nouns. Refer to the examples on the board. Ask, *What one thing do all these words have in common?* (the apostrophe.) Circle the apostrophe. Read the words that end in *-'s.* Note that these nouns form the possessive by adding an apostrophe (') and *s.* Read the words that end in *-s's.* Note that these words already ended with an s, but still also form the possessive by adding an apostrophe (') and *-s* to the final *-s.*

Then point out the plural nouns. Have volunteers say the possessive form. Point out that the plural nouns that end in *-s* add just an apostrophe. (Examples: *boys - boys'; families - families'*). Point out that the plural nouns that **do not** end in *-s add an apostrophe (') and s.* (Examples: *children-children's; sheep-sheep's*).

Scaffolded Verbal Prompting

Use the following verbal prompts to help students better understand possessive nouns.

Nonverbal Prompt for Active Participation

Pre-Production: *Point to (Peter's) book.*

One- or Two-Word Response Prompt

Early Production: *Is this correct: Peter's—P-E-T-E-R-S?*

Prompt for Short Answers to Higher-Level Thinking Skills

Speech Emergence: *How do you say "the pen that belongs to Kathy"?* (Kathy's pen) *How do you spell* Kathy's?

Prompt for Detailed Answers to Higher-Level Thinking Skills

Intermediate and Advanced Fluency: *Listen to these words:* our class's team. *Tell me to whom the team belongs. Whose team is it? Does the team belong to one class or more than one class? How do you say "the cats that belong to the children"?* (the children's cats)

II. DEVELOP GRAMMAR SKILLS IN CONTEXT
Visual/Physical Focus on Grammar Skill

Objective: Develop and demonstrate understanding of possessive nouns.

Materials: Blackline Master 30, crayons, pencils

Whole Group Activity

Brainstorm a list of singular nouns. Make sure that the list includes singular nouns that end in *s,* as well as some that will make irregular plurals. Select words from the list and have volunteers make them plural. Have students underline the plural nouns ending in *-s.* Have other volunteers draw two lines under plural nouns not ending in *-s.* Work together to form the possessive nouns in each category. Have students say the words, then write the correct response. Ask students *who, what,* and *where* questions to elicit information about what nouns are alike and which ones are different.

Small Group Activity

Divide the class into groups of four students of mixed language ability. Have students refer to the noun word bank that they just made for examples. Ask each student to take turns writing or dictating two singular nouns, two plural nouns, two singular possessive nouns, and two plural possessive nouns.

Partner Activity

Extension: Write two or three of the sentences on the chalkboard. Ask a student to circle the possessive noun in the sentence and tell you if it is singular or plural.

The baseball player's coach helped him with his pitching. (player's, singular)

The children's soccer ball went over the fence. (children's, plural)

The horses' saddles were put on before the race. (horses', plural)

Provide each student with a copy of Blackline Master 30. Instruct students to use crayons or pencils when creating their pictures. The partners choose two kinds of things they would like to own or collect. (Examples: CDs, baseball cards.) Have partners draw pictures of themselves with their own collections. Ask partners to explain their pictures to each other. Then have students write the possessive noun showing to whom the item(s) belong. Partners should take turns describing the other's collection. Have them share their work with the class. Compare and contrast the collections, encouraging students to use as many possessive nouns as possible.

Technology Link

Type a list of singular and plural nouns into a word processing program. Pair students of varying language levels. Have students use the computer to form the possessive noun for each word. Then have them spell-check their answers. Set up a two-column table and ask them to use the Cut and Paste function to list the words in two columns: *Singular* and *Plural.*

III. PRACTICE GRAMMAR SKILLS
Written Focus on Grammar Skill

Use Blackline Masters 31 and 32 to reinforce the identification and use of possessive nouns.

Introduce Blackline Master 31: Whose Is It?

Objective: Identify and use possessive nouns.

Materials: Blackline Master 31

[**Answers:** teacher's, players', deer's, school's, women's, player's, children's, classmates']

Form student pairs. Distribute Blackline Master 31. Read aloud and discuss activity directions with students. Complete the first exercise together. Discuss the first illustration. Ask, *Whose is it? Looking at the picture, who owns the apple?* Then ask students to circle the phrase that describes the illustration. Ask pairs to complete the rest of the exercises.

Informal Assessment

Have students turn to page 96 in their textbooks. Read aloud the first sentence in More Practice A. Ask, *Do you hear a possessive noun in this sentence?* Read the sentence again, but use the possessive noun. Repeat the questioning. Ask, *How do you know the noun is now possessive?*

Introduce Blackline Master 32: Complete the Sentences

Objective: Choose singular or plural possessive nouns to complete a sentence.

Materials: Blackline Master 32; pencils

[**Possible Answers:** Joe's, family's, library's, school's, player's, boys']

Form student pairs. Distribute Blackline Master 32. Discuss the illustrations, asking students what the subject of a sentence might be if it were based on each picture. Read aloud and discuss activity directions with students. Make sure students understand the label for each picture. Complete the first exercise together. Ask pairs to complete the rest of the exercises or have the students work independently.

Informal Assessment

Have students turn to page 97, and point to the photo on the page. Ask, *What do you see here? What is the boy doing? Whose soccer ball is it? How might you put those two ideas together to make a sentence? What is the possessive noun in the sentence? Can you make that word plural?*

Use the following chart to assess and reteach.

Are students able to:	
orally identify possessive nouns?	Reteach using the Language Support Activity on TE page 96 for oral practice.
identify possessive nouns in sentence context?	Reteach using the Guided Practice Activity on TE page 96.
distinguish between singular and plural possessive nouns?	Reteach using the Reteach Activity on TE page 97.

My Stuff

Draw a picture of yourself with things you would like to collect or own. Complete the sentence telling who owns the collection.

These things belong to _____. (name)

These are _____ things.

Whose Is It?

Look at the illustration. Circle the correct possessive noun.

the teacher's apple
the teachers' apple

the baseball players' coach
the baseball player's coaches

one deer's antlers
the deers' antlers

the school's flag
the schools' flag

the women's golf bags
the womens' golf bags

the soccer player's ball
the soccer players' ball

the children's zoo
the childrens' zoo

my classmates' backpacks
my classmate's backpacks

Complete the Sentence

Look at the pictures. Read each caption under the picture. Complete each sentence with a possessive noun. Underline each singular possessive noun. Circle each plural possessive noun.

_____ bike club is going on a trip.

The _____ house is at the corner.

Notice that the _____ exit sign is to the right.

Our _____ soccer team won the championship.

The _____ home run made the coach happy.

The _____ photo showed them racing to the finish line.

HOW LANGUAGE CHANGES

Introduce this lesson before Pupil Edition pages 116–117.

I. DEVELOP ORAL LANGUAGE
Oral Focus on Vocabulary Skill

Objective: Orally connect his/her own experiences, information, insights, and ideas with how language changes

Whole Group Oral Language Activity

Ask students which sports they play and which ones they watch on TV. Talk about sports in their home countries. Work with the students to find articles in newspapers and sports magazines about each sport. Write the name for each sport and related words on the chalkboard as you use them and/or read them in print. Point out which words are compounds *(basketball, football, softball)*. Point out words in print, such as *pro* (for *professional*) or *stats* (for *statistics*) that are examples of clipped words.

Display pictures of various types of ethnic foods. Write the name of the country or culture on the board and list the foods. Point out the fact that we borrow the names of these foods from other languages. Explain to students that language is always changing. New words or slang can be formed from joining words together (blended word), from shortening a word (clipped word), from combining two words (compound word), or using words from other languages (borrowed word).

Scaffolded Verbal Prompting

Use the following verbal prompts to help students identify *compound, clipped, blended,* or *borrowed* words.

Nonverbal Prompt for Active Participation

Pre-Production: Act out the two words that form the word *basketball.*

One- or Two-Word Response Prompt

Early Production: *Name a sport. Tell me if you hear two words in that name. Tell me the name of a food that is from another country.*

Prompt for Short Answers to Higher-Level Thinking Skills

Speech Emergence: *Can you name an example of a clipped word? a foreign word?*

Prompt for Detailed Answers to Higher-Level Thinking Skills

Intermediate and Advanced Fluency: *Give me an example of a compound word, a blended word, and a clipped word.*

II. DEVELOP VOCABULARY SKILLS IN CONTEXT
Visual/Physical Focus on Vocabulary Skill

Objective: Orally use structural analysis to identify how language changes.

Small Group Activity
Make four sets of flash cards with the following words: *brunch, motel, smog, phone, plane, bike, campground, notebook, newspaper, rodeo, moccasins,* and *taco.* Display one set on the chalk tray. Use classroom props, objects, or pictures to discuss each word's meaning. Write on the board: *compound words, clipped words, blended words,* and *borrowed words.* Have each group sort the cards, using a dictionary for reference.

Partner Activity
Form student pairs of varying language levels. Provide each with a set of ten index cards. Have each student choose five favorite words from the lesson and make a picture card for each word. Have partners ask yes or no questions in order to try and guess each word.

III. PRACTICE VOCABULARY SKILLS
Written Focus on Vocabulary Skill

Objective: Identify words that are formed in different ways.
Materials: Blackline Master 33; pencils

Introduce Blackline Master 33: Adding To or Taking Away?
Distribute Blackline Master 33. Read aloud the directions, and complete the first exercise together. Have partners work together to complete the rest of the page.

Objective: Locate the meanings, pronunciations, and derivations of unfamiliar words using dictionaries, glossaries, and other sources.
Materials: Blackline Master 34; pencils, dictionaries, map

Introduce Blackline Master 34: How Language Changes
Distribute Blackline Master 34 and a dictionary to each group of students. Read aloud Direction A with students, and complete the first exercise together. Then read aloud Direction B and point out a world map. Use non-adhesive labels or dots to locate the countries listed on the blackline master. Complete the first exercise as a class. Have groups work together to complete the rest of the page.

Informal Assessment
Have students turn to page 117 in the textbook. Read aloud the first exercise in Practice A. Ask, *What word in the sentence is underlined? Tell me if you think this word is a* compound, clipped, blended, *or* borrowed *word.* Continue with other examples.

Use the following chart to assess and reteach.

Are students able to:	
identify compound, clipped, blended, and borrowed words?	Reteach using Reteach Blackline Master 30 on TE page 117.
use prior knowledge and context clues to identify these words?	Reteach using the Language Support Activity on TE page 116.

Name_____ Date_____

Adding To or Taking Away?

Look at the picture or letters. Pay attention to the + or − signs. Add or subtract to build a new word.

smog	basketball	football	motel
mailbox	sweatshirt	brunch	birdhouse

1.  + ◯ = _____

2. + − ABC = _____

3.  + = _____

4.  + = _____

5. + − ABC = _____

6.  + ◯ = _____

7.  + = _____

8.  + − ABC = _____

How Language Changes

A. Read the clue on the left. Match it to one of the words at the right.

1. This word is short for *bicycle*.   pro

2. A word that joins together *post* and *card*.   photo

3. The shortened form of *telephone*.   airplane

4. This word is created by combining *breakfast* and *lunch*. postcard

5. This word is short for *professional*.   homer

6. A word that joins together *air* and *plane*.   phone

7. The shortened form of *home run*.   bike

8. This word is short for *photograph*.   brunch

B. Read each sentence. Read the words in the word box. Choose the correct foreign term from the word box. Write it on the line. Use a dictionary, if necessary.

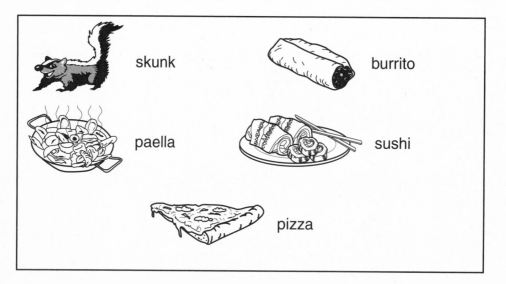

skunk   burrito

paella   sushi

pizza

1. An Italian pie made with cheese and tomato sauce. _____

2. A rice dish from Spain. _____

3. The Algonquin word for a small black and white animal. _____

4. Small pieces of raw fish and rice served in Japanese restaurants. _____

5. A Mexican food of rice with meat or vegetables wrapped in a flour tortilla.

_____

OUTLINING

Introduce this lesson before Pupil Edition pages 118–119.

I. DEVELOP ORAL LANGUAGE
Oral Focus on Composition Skill

Objective: Orally describe and outline a topic.

TPR

Extension: Ask pairs of students to imagine that one lives in the country and one lives in the city. Depending on language proficiency, have them use words or pictures to complete an outline about their lives.

Whole Group Oral Language Activity

Write the following words on non-adhesive labels: *title, main idea, subtopic, details.* Divide the class in two. Tell students they are going to create two different stories: (I.) The life of a horse in the country; (II.) The life of a dog in the city. After they have had time to create their story, have them act out and tell the story to the class. After each story is presented, challenge students to retell facts in order of importance and provide as many details as possible. Write the details of each story on a separate line on a piece of butcher paper. Cut apart each detail into sentence strips. Work with the students to combine the sentence strips into outlines for (I.) The life of a horse and (II.) The life of a dog. Arrange the outlines on the board. As you do, ask questions so that students become familiar with the words: *title, main ideas, subtopics, details.* Brainstorm titles. Complete the outlines with the correct placement of Roman numerals, capital letters, and numbers. Check for comprehension with TPR commands.

Scaffolded Verbal Prompting

Use the following verbal prompts to help students better determine the parts of an outline.

Nonverbal Prompt for Active Participation

Pre-Production: *Look at the outlines. Point to the title. Show me pictures of the two main ideas in the outlines.*

One- or Two-Word Response Prompt

Early Production: *Name the two animals in these outlines. Show me where each of these animals lives in our stories.*

Prompt for Short Answers to Higher-Level Thinking Skills

Speech Emergence: *What are the two main ideas? How many subtopics relate to the first main idea? the second?*

Prompt for Detailed Answers to Higher-Level Thinking Skills

Intermediate and Advanced Fluency: *Why does this section begin with Roman numeral II?*

II. DEVELOP COMPOSITION SKILLS IN CONTEXT
Visual/Physical Focus on Composition Skill

Objective: Listen to learn by taking notes, organizing, and summarizing spoken and visual ideas.

Small Group Activity

Form small groups. Give each a lower-grade social studies text and have them outline a topic.

Partner Activity

Provide each pair of students with a photo essay from a magazine and a set of index cards labeled *title, main ideas, subtopics,* and *details.* Ask students to cut out pictures and words that correspond to each index card. Then have students arrange the cards, pictures, and words into an outline.

Technology Link

Have each group type the outline they create into a word-processing program. Encourage students to use tabs for placement.

III. PRACTICE COMPOSITION SKILLS
Written Focus on Composition Skill

Introduce Blackline Master 35: Parts of an Outline

Objective: Identify the parts of an outline by visual and verbal cues.

Materials: Blackline Master 35

Form student pairs of varying levels. Distribute Blackline Master 35. Review the parts of an outline with the students. Read aloud the activity directions with students. Brainstorm ideas for *What I Do at Home* and *What I Do in School.* Suggest ways to organize their ideas, such as by the time of day or by the type of activity. Have students write or draw activities. Have partners work together to complete the activity. Tell students that they may refer to the outline they've created on the board or on page 118 as models.

Introduce Blackline Master 36: Writing an Outline

Objective: Identify and understand the parts of an outline and their correct placement.

Materials: Blackline Master 36; scissors, pencils, sentence strips, tape, chart paper

Distribute Blackline Master 36. Make a set of sentence strips that match the boxes on the blackline master. Ask student volunteers to hold each strip. Have students give and follow commands by which they arrange the strips into a proper outline form, using the blackline master as a guide. Read aloud the directions with students. Then choose a topic and work together to create a classroom outline. Give students time to write or draw responses in each box. Have volunteers fill in the sentence strips and tape them onto chart paper. Discuss the logical order of the outline and rearrange the strips, if necessary.

Informal Assessment

Have students turn to page 118. Refer to the sample outline. Ask: *How is this outline in the text the same as your outline? How is it different? Tell me what is outlined in A, B, C order? 1, 2, 3 order?*

Use the following chart to assess and reteach.

Are students able to: distinguish main idea, subtopics, and supporting details?	Reteach by matching the sentence strips from Blackline Master 35 to Reteach BLM 31 on TE page 119.
place ideas in an outline in a logical order?	Reteach using the Reteach Activity on TE page 119; provide word/picture cards for pre- and early-production students.

Parts of an Outline

Read the parts of the outline provided as a guide. Think of things you do at home and things you do at school. Use words or pictures to add details to complete the outline.

Title: At Home and at School

I. Things I Do at Home

    A. My Chores

        1. _____

        2. _____

        3. _____

    B. When I Have Fun

        1. _____

        2. _____

        3. _____

II. Things I Do at School

    A. My Work

        1. _____

        2. _____

        3. _____

    B. When I Have Fun

        1. _____

        2. _____

        3. _____

Writing an Outline

Cut out the boxes. Use the boxes to build an outline.

Title:

I. main idea:

   A. subtopic:

      1. detail:

      2. detail:

   B. subtopic:

      1. detail:

      2. detail:

II. main idea:

   A. subtopic:

      1. detail:

      2. detail:

   B. subtopic:

      1. detail:

      2. detail:

Introduce this lesson before Pupil Edition pages 124–143.

I. PREWRITE
Oral Warm Up

Objectives:
- Connect own experiences, information, insights, and ideas with experiences of others through speaking and listening.
- Compare own perception with the perceptions of others.

TPR

Whole Group Oral Language Activity

Compare two families that appear on popular family-oriented television shows, either sitcoms or dramas. Provide copies of pictures of families as they appear in magazines or the newspaper. If possible compare a television family with a family in a book recently read by the class. Have students name the people, places, and events that are the same and different in each family.

Draw a T-chart on the board. Label each column with the name of each family chosen. Transcribe or post the information about each family in the correct column. Ask volunteers to compose sentences, draw, or cut out pictures from the newspapers and magazines about the people, places, and events in each family's lives. Continue with questions and answers to help students compare how the families are alike or different.

Graphic Organizer

Objectives:
- Begin prewriting for writing that compares
- Use a graphic organizer to record ideas

Introduce the Writing Mode

Tell students that writing that compares shows how two things are the same and how they are different. When they discussed the two families, they were making comparisons. Using the chart on the board, model writing that compares. Have volunteers add other sentences about the two families based on the information displayed on the chart.

Scaffolded Writing Instruction

Pre-Production and Early Production

Blackline Master 37

Speech Emergence

Using Blackline Master 37, have students work in pairs to complete the chart. Allow students to draw their answers.

Have students work in pairs. Ask students to draw pictures on their T-charts. Encourage them to label their pictures.

Intermediate and Advanced Fluency

Have students work in pairs. Ask them to name the people and to write sentences that compare the families.

Research and Inquiry: Use Parts of a Book

Make sets of word cards for each pair: *Table of Contents, chapter, title, page number,* and *index.* Refer to a nonfiction book of your choice. Point out the Table of Contents, chapters, title, page numbers, and index. Have volunteers match the word card to the correct section of the book. Give each pair of students a different book. Ask them to match the word cards to the correct section in their book, then share their findings with the class.

II. DRAFT

Focus on Writing That Compares

Objectives:
• Identify similarities and differences and organize ideas accordingly.
• Begin drafting writing that compares.
TPR

Begin by asking students to help you write about two families with which they are familiar; for example, two families from popular TV shows. List facts about them under each show's name. Then have students draw a line from an item in Program A that they can compare to an item in Program B. Begin to make comparisons by moving back and forth from one family to the other. Point out the words used to describe comparisons.

Scaffolded Writing Instruction

Pre-Production and Early Production
Blackline Master 38

Use Blackline Master 38 to help students organize sets of items that they compared on Blackline Master 37 or in class. Ask them to cut out pictures from Blackline Master 37, or draw items discussed in class. Have them line these up item by item on Blackline Master 38, or they can draw representations. Encourage them to add other items.

Speech Emergence
Blackline Master 39

Use Blackline Master 39 to help students organize sets of items that they compared on Blackline Master 37 or in class. Before they paste in pictures or write in words or phrases for comparison, ask *who, what, where, why,* or *how* questions about each family in order to prompt the comparisons. (Examples: *Which family is funnier? Which family has the most pets?*) Have students add words of comparison.

Intermediate and Advanced Fluency

Students may begin composing their writing that compares. Brainstorm what items students can compare. (Examples: people, places, events, type of programs, likes and dislikes.) Suggest they use a Venn diagram to organize their ideas. List items about each family under the families' names. Point out the common section in a Venn diagram and explain that they use this section for items that are the same about each family. Review the features of writing that compares. Suggest that students state the main idea in the first paragraph. Then, in the following paragraphs they can add supporting details that show similarities and differences. Remind them that their writing should not jump from one comparison to another.

III. REVISE

Objectives:
- Revise writing that compares
- Add details to elaborate

TPR

Pre-Production and Early
Production
Blackline Master 38
Speech Emergence
Blackline Master 39

Intermediate and Advanced
Fluency

Focus on Elaboration
Display a brand new pencil and an obviously used pencil. Write the following sentences on the board and read them aloud to the class:

I have a pencil. I have another pencil.

Have volunteers elaborate on each sentence by adding details that help the reader identify which pencil is being described. Ask students to use words that compare. Make a word bank of comparison words *(both, but, too, also, like, as)*. Read the sentences and have students raise their hands when they hear comparison words.

Scaffolded Instruction for Revising
Use students' work in Blackline Master 38 to help them understand the concept of elaboration. Ask them to draw more details.

Use students' work in Blackline Master 39 to help them elaborate on which items are similar and which are different. Ask them to add other items of comparison.

Students may elaborate on their writing by adding details and comparison words.

Technology Link
Have partners type their ideas for their writing that compares in a computer. Have them practice using the Cut and Paste function to put supporting details that show similarities in one paragraph and supporting details that show differences in another paragraph.

IV. REVISE • PEER CONFERENCING

Objectives:
- Participate in peer conferences.
- Give and receive constructive feedback.
- Revise a writing that compares.

Focus on Peer Conferencing
Form groups of varied language levels for peer conferencing. Have the more fluent students review with the pre- and early-production students what they have compared in their illustrations. Have the more fluent students share their writing with the pre- and early-production students. Encourage the students with limited proficiency to ask *who, what, where,* and *how* questions.

Using page 137 as your guide, prepare checklists for each proficiency level and write these on the chalkboard, so students may refer to them as they engage in a conference.

V. PROOFREADING
Focus on English Conventions

Objectives:
• Demonstrate comprehension of proofreading strategies.
• Identify and use correct forms of singular and plural nouns.

Objectives: Develop and demonstrate understanding of forming plural nouns.
Materials: Blackline Master 40, pencils, a dictionary
[**Answers: A.** 1. house 2. programs 3. deer 4. children, movie 5. Fish 6. family **B.** answers will vary]

Write this on the chalkboard:

You are comparing two television shows. Do you call them program or programs?

Tell students that nouns that name more than one person, place, thing, or idea are plural nouns. Most plural nouns, add *-s* or *-es*. Remind students that not all words form the plural by just adding *-s*. Refer students back to pages 88–89. (Examples: leaf/leaves; piano/pianos; deer/deer)

Ask students to complete Blackline Master 40 for extra practice on the grammar skill, before looking back at their work and identifying which nouns are incorrectly formed. Model using a dictionary, if necessary.

VI. PUBLISH

Objective:
• Present a neat final copy of writing that compares.

TPR
Extension: You might have individuals write ads promoting and explaining the video documentary, as though it would appear as an entry in a television program guide.

Using page 140 as your guide, prepare a checklist for each proficiency level and write these on the chalkboard, so students may refer to them as they prepare the final version of their writing that compares.

Create a Video
If possible, have the class prepare a video documentary that compares one family with another. Work with students to arrange the order of the presentation. Select the more fluent students to be the on-camera commentators. Use the illustrations drawn by the students as inserts. Brainstorm a title, such as *What Makes A Family?*

VII. LISTENING, SPEAKING, VIEWING, REPRESENTING

TPR

Adapt the steps on pages 142–143 to generate activities that will bring out the talents of all students, including those that are in the pre- and early-production stages. Have these students rehearse what they might show and say in their final presentations.

Informal Assessment
When assessing students' learning, you need to adapt your expectations of what constitutes an appropriate presentation. For example, you may wish to have them use pantomime to compare two items.

Name_____ Date_____

T-Chart

Label the two boxes at the top. Draw pictures of things that are similar and different in the correct column. Write words that compare and contrast each family. Add details to help make the comparison.

Sit-com Comparison

Write the name of each family in the TV screen. Draw or write details about the people, places, and events in each program's family. Match the two items that you want to compare. Circle the correct word: same/different.

Same/Different

Same/Different

Same/Different

Same/Different

Venn Diagram

Write the name of each family on the correct line. Make comparisons. Think about what is the same and what is different about the families. Write what is different about family 1 in the left circle. Write what is different about family 2 in the right circle. Write what is the same under *Both*.

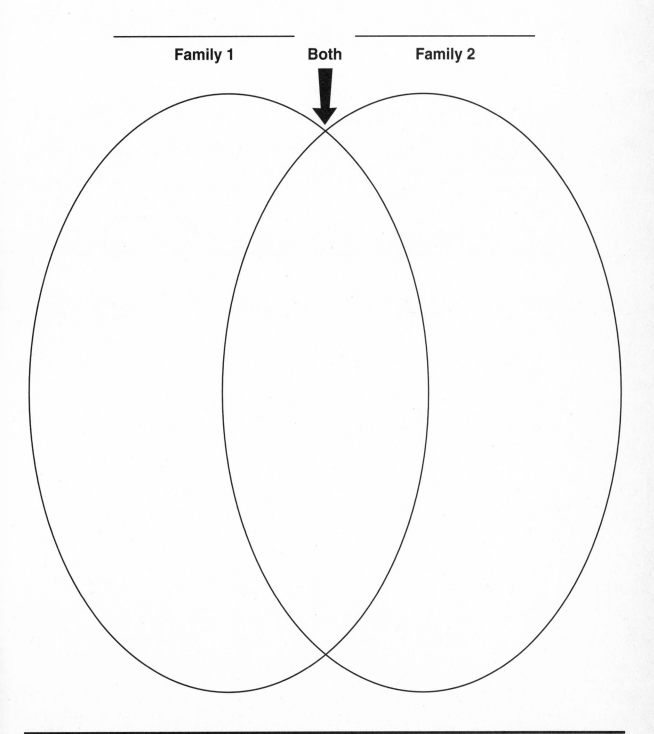

Family 1   **Both**   **Family 2**

Mohammed's House

Part A.
Look at the picture. Circle the correct word.

1. This is Mohammed's house/houses.

2. There are two different program/programs/program's on TV.

3. The parent/parents are watching deer/deers on *Wildlife.*

4. The child/children are watching a movie/movies.

5. The movie's name is *Attack of the Killer Fish/Fishes.*

6. Is Mohammed's family/families the same as your family?

Part B.

7. How is Mohammed's family the same as, or different from, your family?

_____

_____

_____

_____

8. Circle the plural forms of nouns in your writing.

I. DEVELOP ORAL LANGUAGE
Oral Focus on Grammar Skill

Objective: Orally identify action verbs and use different verb tenses.

Whole Group Oral Language Activity

Invite students to look at the photograph on page 177. Ask: *What do you think the man in the picture is doing?* After some discussion, explain that the man is Jackson Pollock, a famous artist, who often painted large canvases on the floor. Write the sentence *He paints pictures* on the chalkboard. Underline the word *paint.* Remind students that words that tell what the subject of a sentence does, such as *paint,* are called *action verbs.* Write the words *Action Verbs* on the chalkboard. Ask: *What are some things you like to do?* Record a list of responses in the present tense.

Ask volunteers to name some things they do every day. Record a response that is expressed in the present tense such as *I play soccer.* Explain that verbs in the *present tense* tell what usually happens. Then ask volunteers to tell some things they did yesterday. Record a response that is expressed in the past tense such as *I visited a friend.* Explain that verbs in the *past tense* show what has already happened. Many past tense verbs end in *-ed.* Ask students to tell what they will do when they get home from school today. Record a response such as *I will eat a snack.* Explain that verbs in the *future tense* show action that will happen later. Verbs in the future tense include the word *will* or sometimes *shall.* Invite students to use the action verbs from the list to make up sentences telling what they usually do, what they did yesterday, and what they will do tomorrow.

Scaffolded Verbal Prompting

TPR

Use the following verbal prompts to help students better understand verb tenses.

Nonverbal Prompt for Active Participation

Pre-Production: *Look at the picture. Point to the man. Now show me what he does.*

One- or Two-Word Response Prompt

Early Production: *Who is in the picture? Tell me something he does.*

Prompt for Short Answers to Higher-Level Thinking Skills

Speech Emergence: *Tell me who is in the picture. What does the person do? Which word tells what he does?*

Prompt for Detailed Answers to Higher-Level Thinking Skills

Intermediate and Advanced Fluency: *Tell me, in one sentence, what the man in the picture does. Repeat the sentence once more. Which word in the sentence is an action verb? Is the verb in the present, past, or future tense?*

II. DEVELOP GRAMMAR SKILLS IN CONTEXT
Visual/Physical Focus on Grammar Skill

Objective: Develop and demonstrate understanding of verb tenses.

Materials: Blackline Master 41, scissors

TPR

Whole Group Activity

Write a sentence on the chalkboard such as, *Kate picks flowers in the spring.* Underline the word *picks.* Provide each student with a copy of Blackline Master 41. Instruct students to cut out each card. Then invite students to hold up the "present" card when they hear a verb in the present tense, the "past" card when they hear a verb in the past tense, and the "future" card when they hear a verb in the future tense. Invite volunteers to read aloud each verb as students hold up the correct card. Repeat with other sentences.

Small Group Activity

Ask students to think of creative activities they know how to do. *(I paint pictures. I bake cakes. I play the piano.)* Ask student volunteers to take turns acting out a creative activity. Invite students to guess each activity. Then invite volunteers to make up sentences about each activity using the present, past, and future tenses.

Extension: Write two or three of the sentences on the chalkboard. Ask a student to underline the action verb in the sentence. Then have them tell whether the verb is written in the present, past, or future tense.

Extension: Students can make up sentences using each verb as it is written. Have the students read the sentences to their partners. Challenge partners to think of new sentences, this time changing the tense of the verb.

Partner Activity

Make a list of about ten action verbs that show a creative activity, such as *perform, paint, play, act, cook, plant,* and *dance.* Write the verbs individually on index cards varying the tense used. Have partners lay the cards facedown between them. Model for students how to draw a card, read the word, and tell whether the word is written in the present, past, or future tense. Have partners take turns doing the activity independently until all cards are used.

Technology Link

Type a simple sentence containing a present-tense verb into a word processing program. Pair students of varying language levels. Have students use the computer to make three copies of the sentence. Then have them change the verb in the second sentence to the past tense and the verb in the third sentence to the future tense. Ask them to check that all the sentences make sense with the changed verb by reading each one aloud.

III. PRACTICE GRAMMAR SKILLS
Written Focus on Grammar Skill

Use Blackline Masters 42 and 43 to reinforce identification and use of past, present, and future verb tenses.

Introduce Blackline Master 42: Now, Then, and Later

Objective: Identify and use past, present, and future verb tenses.

Materials: Blackline Master 42; pencils and markers

Have students recall some of the activities they do every day, as they discussed earlier in the lesson. Distribute Blackline Master 42. Read aloud and discuss the directions with students. Explain that they should draw pictures showing one activity for each box: one in the present, one in the past, and one in the future. Read the incomplete sentences and tell students they should fill in the blank with the correct verb tense for each activity they have drawn. You may ask volunteers to give examples of how each sentence can be completed.

Informal Assessment

Have students turn to page 169 in their textbooks. Read aloud a sentence from More Practice A. Ask, *What is the action verb in the sentence? How do you know? What is the tense of the verb? How can you tell?*

Introduce Blackline Master 43: Ready, Set, Action!

Objective: Choose verbs to form logical sentences and identify correct verb tenses.

Materials: Blackline Master 43; pencils

[**Answers:** 1. will finish, future; 2. played, past; 3. planted, past; 4. cooks, present]

Form student pairs. Distribute Blackline Master 43. Discuss the illustrations, asking students what the people in the pictures might be doing. Read aloud and discuss activity directions with students, as well as the words in the box. Complete the first exercise together. Ask pairs to complete the rest of the exercises.

Informal Assessment

Have students turn to page 177, and point to the photo. Ask, *What do you see here? What words could you use to describe it? How might you put those words together to make a sentence? What is the action verb in the sentence? What is the tense of the verb in the sentence?*

Use the following chart to assess and reteach.

Are students able to: orally describe the contents of a picture?	Reteach using the Language Support Activity on TE page 164 for oral practice.
put together words to make sentences?	Reteach using the Language Support Activity on TE page 168.
identify verbs and verb tenses?	Reteach using the Reteach Activity on TE page 169.

When Was the Action?

Cut out the three cards. Hold up the correct card as you hear each word.

Past

Present

Future

Now, Then, and Later

Read the verb tense in each box. Draw a picture to show something you do today, you did yesterday, and you will do tomorrow. Write a verb to complete each sentence.

Present

Today, I _____ .

Past

Yesterday, I _____ .

Future

Tomorrow, I will _____ .

Ready, Set, Action!

Look at the pictures. Read each sentence. Use the words from the word box to complete each sentence. Circle, *Past, Present,* or *Future* to show the tense of each verb.

planted	played	cooks	will finish

1. Olivia _____ her homework this evening.

Past   Present   Future

2. Tyler _____ Abraham Lincoln on President's Day.

Past   Present   Future

3. Abby _____ a pine tree on Earth Day.

Past   Present   Future

4. Mr. Vasquez _____ breakfast for his family every morning.

Past   Present   Future

SUBJECT-VERB AGREEMENT

I. DEVELOP ORAL LANGUAGE
Oral Focus on Grammar Skill

Objective: Orally describe pictures and identify subjects and verbs that agree.

Whole Group Oral Language Activity

Invite students to look at the photograph on page 188. Ask: *Who is in the picture?* (a boy and a girl) *What are they doing?* (dancing) *How many children are in the picture?* (two) Write the following sentences on the chalkboard and read each one aloud: *The boy dances. The girl dances. The boy and girl dance.* Ask volunteers to name the subject in each sentence. (boy; girl; boy and girl) Ask volunteers to name the verbs in each sentence. (dance; dance; dances) Explain that the subject and verb must always work together, or agree.

Underline and read aloud the subject in the first sentence. Ask: *Is the subject singular or plural?* (singular) Tell the class that a singular subject such as *boy* must have a verb that works with a singular subject. Underline and read aloud the verb *dances.* Tell the class that present-tense verbs that work with singular subjects end in *-s* or *-es.* Underline and read aloud the subject in the third sentence. Ask: *Is the subject singular or plural?* (plural) Tell the class that a sentence with a plural subject must have a verb that works with it. Underline and read aloud the verb *dance.* Explain that verbs in the present tense that work with plural subjects do not add an end in *-s* or *-es.* Have volunteers say each sentence aloud to hear whether they agree.

Scaffolded Verbal Prompting

Use the following verbal prompts to help students better understand subject-verb agreement.

Nonverbal Prompt for Active Participation

Pre-Production: *Look at the picture. Point to the people. Show me on your hands how many there are. Show me what they do.*

One- or Two-Word Response Prompt

Early Production: *Tell me how many people are in the picture. What does the boy do? What do both children do?*

Prompt for Short Answers to Higher-Level Thinking Skills

Speech Emergence: *Name the people in the picture. Tell me what they do. Name the verb that tells what they do.*

Prompt for Detailed Answers to Higher-Level Thinking Skills

Intermediate and Advanced Fluency: *Tell me, in one sentence, who is in the picture and what they are doing. Repeat the sentence in the present tense. Name the subject of the sentence. Name the verb in the sentence. Tell whether the subject and verb agree.*

II. DEVELOP GRAMMAR SKILLS IN CONTEXT
Visual/Physical Focus on Grammar Skill

Objective: Develop and demonstrate understanding of subject-verb agreement.

Materials: Blackline Master 44

TPR

Extension: Help students practice using negative contractions as a part of the verb in a sentence. Ask students for examples of activities they do not like to do. On the board write a sentence to model:

I **do not** _____. *He/she* **does not** _____. *They* **do not** _____.

Ask volunteers to choose a verb to place in the sentence and say the sentence with the correct contraction.

Example: I don't cook.

Whole Group Activity

Ask students to discuss things they like to do to express themselves. Invite a volunteer to act out something he or she likes to do. Have students guess what the volunteer is doing. Then write a present-tense sentence on the chalkboard that corresponds with the activity, leaving a blank for the verb. For example: *Carlos _____ books.* Then ask students to complete the sentence with the correct verb choice. Repeat with other examples.

Small Group Activity

Make a list of simple sentences with both singular and plural subjects and verbs that show personal expression—some should agree and some should not agree. For example: *The girl sings; The friends dances; Lisa draw; The brothers perform.* Distribute copies of the lists to groups. Organize students into groups and distribute Blackline Master 44. Have students cut out each card. Then invite a volunteer to read a sentence from the list. Ask others in the group to choose the "thumbs up" card when they hear subjects and verbs that agree and to choose the "thumbs down" card when they hear subjects and verbs that do not agree. After students have chosen, have them hold up their cards at the same time. If students are not all holding the same card, have them discuss why they think as they do, and try to reach a consensus as a group. Repeat the activity with each sentence.

Partner Activity

Make a list of ten subjects and ten verbs that agree and write them on the chalkboard. Use both singular and plural subjects and verbs. Distribute 20 small index cards for each pair of students and have one partner write the subjects—one on each card, as the other partner writes the verbs. Tell students they will play a game similar to Old Maid called "Odd Verb" with the cards. Have the pairs shuffle the cards and deal the cards to each partner. Each player should pair any subject and verb cards that agree and remove them from their hand. Then have each partner take turns drawing a card from the other player's hand. Players should see if the new card can be paired correctly with a subject or verb in his or her hand. If so, they should remove that pair. Continue playing until one partner has paired all of his or her cards.

Technology Link

Type several simple present-tense sentences into a word processing program, such as *The girl writes poetry.* Pair students of varying language levels. Have students use the computer to change the subjects from the singular to their plural forms. Then tell them they must change the verbs so that they agree with the subjects. Ask them to read the new sentences aloud.

III. PRACTICE GRAMMAR SKILLS
Written Focus on Grammar Skill

Use Blackline Masters 45 and 46 to reinforce understanding of subject-verb agreement.

Introduce Blackline Master 45: We Agree!

Objective: Choose sentences that contain correct subject-verb agreement.

Materials: Blackline Master 45; scissors; glue or paste

[**Answers:** The kittens sleep. Oscar draws. The girls race. Mrs. James performs.]

Organize students into groups and distribute Blackline Master 45. Explain to students that they should take turns reading aloud the two sentences that correspond with each picture, as the others in the group listen for subject-verb agreement. Together have the students decide which sentence contains the correct subject-verb agreement. When students have finished the exercise, have them each turn their paper over and draw a picture and write a corresponding simple sentence that contains correct subject-verb agreement. Then have them share their pictures and read their sentences aloud.

Informal Assessment

Have students turn to page 170 in their textbooks. Read aloud a sentence from More Practice B. Ask, *How would you change the subject to make it singular? How would you change the verb to make it agree with the subject?*

Introduce Blackline Master 46: Mix and Match

Objective: Find subjects and verbs that agree and form sentences.

Materials: Blackline Master 46; red and blue crayons

Form student pairs. Distribute Blackline Master 46. Read the words in the boxes aloud with students. Explain that some of the words are subjects and some of the words are verbs, but that they are mixed up. Read aloud and discuss activity directions with students. Model the activity with a volunteer, showing students how to match a subject and a verb that agrees. Explain that more than one verb might work with each subject. Write an example sentence on the chalkboard, such as *Kate and Lily sing a song.* Have partners work together to complete the exercise.

Informal Assessment

Have students turn to page 188, and point to the photo on the page. Ask, *What do you see here?* Say this sentence aloud: *The boy dances with the girl.* Ask: *Is the subject of the sentence singular or plural? What is the verb in the sentence? Do the subject and verb agree? How can you tell?*

Use the following chart to assess and reteach.

Are students able to:	
make a simple sentence that describes the contents of a picture?	Reteach using the Language Support Activity on TE page 170 for oral practice.
identify the simple subject and the verb of a sentence?	Reteach using the Hands-On Activity on TE page 164b.
tell whether the subject and verb agree?	Reteach using the Reteach Activity on TE page 171.

Thumbs Up, Thumbs Down

Read each card. Cut out each card.

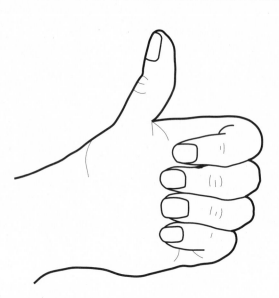

Subject and verb agree.

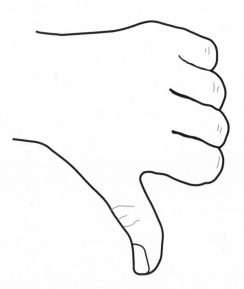

Subject and verb do not agree.

We Agree!

Look at the pictures. Read the sentences aloud and listen for subject-verb agreement. Underline the sentence with the correct subject-verb agreement.

The kittens sleep.

The kittens sleeps.

Oscar draw.

Oscar draws.

The girls race.

The girls races.

Mrs. James perform.

Mrs. James performs.

Mix and Match

Cut out the words below. Separate the subjects and verbs; color the subjects red and the verbs blue. Pair subjects and verbs that agree. Write sentences with words that agree.

puppy	plays	Kate and Lily
teacher	sing	decorate
Matthew	jumps	boys
recites	musician	Mr. Berger

I. DEVELOP ORAL LANGUAGE
Oral Focus on Grammar Skill

Objective: Orally describe actions and identify progressive forms of verbs.

Whole Group Oral Language Activity

Stand before the class with a chair beside you. Say this sentence aloud: *I am standing.* Then sit down and ask: What am I doing now? (Students should indicate that you are sitting.) Write these sentences on the chalkboard: *I am standing* and *I am sitting.* Underline the verb phrases *am standing* and *am sitting.* Tell students that the present-progressive form of the verb tells about an action that is happening right now. Invite a volunteer to stand. Ask the class: *What is (the student) doing?* (Students should indicate that the student is standing.) Then have the volunteer sit down and ask: *What is (the student) doing now?* (The class should indicate that he or she is sitting.) Now invite everyone to stand. Ask: *What are we doing?* (We are standing.) Add the sentence to those on the board, underlining the verb phrase *are standing.* Tell students that the present-progressive form uses the helping verb *am, is* or *are* followed by a verb that ends in *-ing.*

Invite the class to sit back down. Then ask: *What were we doing before we stood?* (We were sitting.) Write the sentence *We were sitting* on the chalkboard. Tell students that the past-progressive form of a verb tells about an action that happened at an earlier time. Invite a volunteer to stand back up. Ask: *What were you doing before you stood?* (I was sitting). Add the new sentences to the chalkboard underlining the verb phrases *were sitting,* and *was sitting.* Explain that the past-progressive form of the verb uses *was* or *were* followed by a verb that ends in *-ing.*

Scaffolded Verbal Prompting

Use the following verbal prompts to help students better understand present progressive and past progressive verbs.

Nonverbal Prompt for Active Participation

Pre-Production: (gesture as you say the following and encourage student participation.) *We are standing up. Now we are sitting down. We are raising our hands. We are putting our hands down.*

One- or Two-Word Response Prompt

Early Production: (Gesture as you say the following. Encourage students to repeat after you.) *Tell me whether you are standing or sitting.* (Point to another student.) *Tell me if he or she is standing or sitting.*

Prompt for Short Answers to Higher-Level Thinking Skills

Speech Emergence: *Please stand up. Are you standing or sitting? Now sit down. Tell me what you are doing now.*

Prompt for Detailed Answers to Higher-Level Thinking Skills

Intermediate and Advanced Fluency: *Stand up and tell me, in one sentence, what you are doing right now. Tell me what you were doing before you stood. What form of the verb tells me what you are doing now? What form tells me what you were doing earlier?*

II. DEVELOP GRAMMAR SKILLS IN CONTEXT
Visual/Physical Focus on Grammar Skill

Objective: Develop and demonstrate understanding of progressive forms of verbs.

Materials: Blackline Master 47, scissors

TPR

Whole Group Activity

Invite students to recall some of the action verbs they used that showed creative expression, such as *paint, dance, perform, play,* and list the verbs on the chalkboard. Invite a volunteer to stand and act out one of the actions. Invite another volunteer to tell what the student is doing. Tell students they should use the present progressive form of the verb to tell what each performer is doing at that moment. After the performer sits down, have another volunteer use the past-progressive form to tell what the student was doing previously. Have students take turns acting out and saying the present-progressive and past-progressive verb forms.

Small Group Activity

Provide cards on which you have written the following verb phrases: *am making; are painting; is reading; are playing,* along with separate cards on which you have written the following subjects: *I; she; he; we; you; they.* Distribute a set of cards to each group and challenge the groups to use subjects and verb phrases together to form complete sentences, such as *I am making a mask.* Have one student in the group record the sentences. Groups may then draw pictures to illustrate the sentences and share them with the class.

Extension: Have students use the past-progressive forms of the verbs shown on the cards to play *What Was I Doing?*

Partner Activity

Tell students they are going to play a game called *What Am I Doing?* Provide pairs of students with Blackline Master 47. Instruct students to cut out each card. Explain that after the cards have been cut out, the cards should be shuffled and placed face down between partners. Have one student draw a card and act out the action shown on the card, and ask, *What am I doing?* The partner should respond with a sentence using the verb in the present-progressive form, such as *You are painting.* Model the game using a student volunteer, if necessary. Instruct students to take turns drawing cards and performing and guessing the action.

Technology Link

Type sentences 6 and 8 from More Practice A on page 179 into a word processing program. Have students use the computer to change the present-progressive form of the verb to the past-progressive, and the past-progressive form to the present-progressive. Ask students to tell which of the actions is happening now and which was happening in the past.

III. PRACTICE GRAMMAR SKILLS
Written Focus on Grammar Skill

Use Blackline Masters 48 and 49 to reinforce understanding and use of present-progressive and past-progressive verb forms.

Introduce Blackline Master 48: Yesterday or Today?

Objective: Recognize present-progressive and past-progressive verb forms.

Materials: Blackline Master 48; pencils

[**Answers:** 1. are debating, today; 2. was thinking, yesterday; 3. were cooking, yesterday; 4. is conducting, today]

Together with students, look at the pictures on Blackline Master 48. Explain that the pictures show actions that are either continuing now or that continued for a time in the past. Pair students of varying language proficiencies. Read aloud and discuss the directions with students. Complete one exercise together, discussing the picture, reading the sentence, and deciding whether the action took place yesterday or today. Have pairs work together to complete the rest of the exercises.

Informal Assessment

Have students turn to page 179 in their textbooks. Read aloud a sentence from More Practice A. Ask, *Does this sentence tell what is happening now,* or *what was happening in the past? Name the verb phrase that tells you.* Repeat the questioning with other sentences.

Introduce Blackline Master 49: Now and Then

Objective: Recognize present-progressive and past-progressive verb forms and write sentences using them.

Materials: Blackline Master 49; pencils

Distribute Blackline Master 49. Discuss the illustrations, explaining that the first picture in each pair shows what is happening now, and the second picture shows what was happening in the past. Read aloud and discuss activity directions with students, as well as the verb phrases in the word box. Complete the first exercise together. Ask pairs to complete the rest of the exercises.

Informal Assessment

Have students turn to page 185, and point to the photo on the page. Ask, *What is happening in the picture? How would you form a sentence to tell that the action is happening now? How would you say the sentence differently if the action had taken place earlier? What are the verb phrases you used in the sentences?*

Use the following chart to assess and reteach.

Are students able to:	
orally describe the actions of self or another individual?	Reteach using the Guided Practice Activity on TE page 178 for oral practice.
distinguish an action that is happening now as opposed to an action that was happening in the past?	Reteach using the Language Support Activity on TE page 178.
identify progressive forms, both present and past?	Reteach using the Reteach Activity on TE page 179.

What Am I Doing?

Cut out each card. Place the cards in a pile face down. Draw a card and perform the action for your partner. Ask: *What am I doing?* Your partner should use the present-progressive form of the verb. Take turns performing and guessing the action.

Yesterday or Today?

Look at the pictures. Read the sentences. Underline the progressive form of the verb. Tell whether the action happened today or yesterday by circling the correct word.

1. Anne and Sylvia are debating.

Yesterday   Today

2. Hans was thinking.

Yesterday   Today

3. On Monday, Eleanor and Seth were cooking.

Yesterday   Today

4. Mr. Bertelucci is conducting.

Yesterday   Today

Name_____ Date_____

Now and Then

Look at the pictures. Read the verb phrases listed in the box. Write a sentence that tells what is happening *now* with the present-progressive form. Write a second sentence telling what was happening *then* with the past-progressive form.

is playing was playing	is painting was painting	are acting were acting

_____

_____

_____

_____

_____

_____

I. DEVELOP ORAL LANGUAGE
Oral Focus on Grammar Skill

Objective: Orally describe pictures and identify regular and irregular verb forms.

Whole Group Oral Language Activity

Remind students that in this unit, we have been using verbs that show expressive action. Invite volunteers to name a few of them. (dance, perform, sing, draw) Write the words *Present, Past,* and *Past Participle* on the chalkboard. Tell the class that *regular verbs* are verbs that have the same spelling in the past and past participle forms. Invite students to look at the picture on page 185. Ask: What does the boy do? (He paints.) Write the word *paint* under the heading *Present*. Ask: *How do we change the ending of a regular verb to show the past tense?* (add *-ed*) Write the word *painted* under the heading *Past*. Explain that a helping verb, such as *has* or *have,* is used with the past participle. Write the word *painted* under the *Past Participle* heading. Write the heading *Regular Verbs* above the chart. Invite students to repeat the three forms after you. Tell students that the past participle is always used with the helping verb *had* to express an action before a certain time in the past. For example: *Susan baked a pie today. She had never baked one before.*

Have students look at the picture on page 187. Ask: What is the girl doing? (She is making a pot.) Write the word *make* in the *Present* column. Ask: *What is the past tense of* make? (made) *What is the past participle?* (made). Write the words under their appropriate headings. Write the heading *Irregular Verbs* above this chart.

Scaffolded Verbal Prompting

Use the following verbal prompts to help students better understand irregular verbs.

Nonverbal Prompt for Active Participation

Pre-Production: *Look at the picture. Point to a person. Now show me what that person did.*

One- or Two-Word Response Prompt

Early Production: *Name a person in the picture. Tell me what he (or she) does. Tell me what they did.*

Prompt for Short Answers to Higher-Level Thinking Skills

Speech Emergence: *Tell me who is in the picture. What does the person do? What verb did you use to tell what he (or she) does? What is the past tense of the verb? What is the past participle?*

Prompt for Detailed Answers to Higher-Level Thinking Skills

Intermediate and Advanced Fluency: *Tell me what you see in the picture. What present-tense verb tells you what he (or she) does? What is the past tense of the verb? Is the verb regular or irregular?*

II. DEVELOP GRAMMAR SKILLS IN CONTEXT
Visual/Physical Focus on Grammar Skill

Objective: Develop and demonstrate understanding of regular and irregular verb forms.

Materials: Blackline Master 50, scissors

TPR

Extension: Students can use the verbs to write pairs of simple rhyming sentences. For example: Madeline had grown. Madeline had thrown. *or* Alex drove. Alex dove. Invite partners read their sentences aloud and listen for the similar verbs.

Whole Group Activity

Make a t-chart with the headings *Regular Verbs* and *Irregular Verbs* and place it in front of the class. Distribute Blackline Master 50 to each student and discuss the pictures on the page. Ask: *What is shown here?* (Things we do with our hands.) Point out that the verb that names the action is written below the picture. Explain that some of the verbs are regular and some are irregular. Have the students cut out all of the pictures. Invite a volunteer to bring one of the pictures to the front of the class. Discuss the picture and the verb with the class, inviting the group to model the activity with their hands. Invite a volunteer to read the past and past participle forms of the verb, and decide whether the verb is regular or irregular. Have the volunteer paste the picture on the t-chart under the correct heading while students group their own pictures into two groups at their desks. Take turns with other volunteers until all the pictures are represented on the chart.

Small Group Activity

Make a list of regular and irregular verbs. Organize the class into teams of three or four students of varying language proficiencies, and give each group a copy of the list. Have a volunteer read one of the verbs aloud. Ask the groups to vote on whether the verb is regular or irregular and have a volunteer record the votes. Then have members of the group work together to write each verb's past and past participle forms. After the forms are read aloud, have the group vote again on whether the verb is regular or irregular, and record their final answers. Did the answers change? Bring the groups together to discuss their results.

Partner Activity

Write the following irregular verbs on index cards: *break, speak, drive, dive, grow, throw, choose, freeze, teach, write, ride.* Mix up the cards and distribute a set to each pair of students. Tell students that some irregular verbs form their principal parts in similar ways. Have partners work together to write the past and past participle of the verbs on the cards. Then have them look for patterns in spelling changes and pair the verbs that change their spelling in similar ways. Have partners continue the activity independently until all the cards are paired.

Technology Link

Type two sentences that contain irregular verbs with incorrect forms such as *Molly writed an essay* and *Sam had rode his horse.* Pair students of varying language levels. Have students use the computer to change the verbs to the correct tense.

III. PRACTICE GRAMMAR SKILLS
Written Focus on Grammar Skill

Use Blackline Masters 51 and 52 to reinforce identification and use of the correct forms of irregular verbs.

Introduce Blackline Master 51: It's Highly Irregular!

Objective: Complete sentences with the correct form of irregular verbs.

Materials: Blackline Master 51; pencils

[Answers: 1. begin, began, begun; 2. swim, swam, swum; 3. eat, ate, eaten; 4. ring, rang, rung; 5. take, took, taken]

Pair students of varying language levels. Distribute Blackline Master 51. Discuss the pictures on the page, pointing out that the situations are not likely to happen. Have students tell what the verbs of a sentence might be if it were based on each picture. Read aloud and discuss activity directions with students, as well as the verbs below each picture. Complete first exercise together. Have partners work together to complete the rest of the exercises.

Informal Assessment

Have students turn to page 184 in their textbooks. Choose a sentence from More Practice A and read it aloud using the incorrect verb form verb. Then read the same sentence using the correct form. Ask, *Which sentence is correct?* Repeat the sentences if necessary. Then choose another sentence and repeat the activity.

Introduce Blackline Master 52: Irregular Verb Mix-up

Objective: Identify and choose correct forms of irregular verbs.

Materials: Blackline Master 52; scissors; glue, paper

[Answers: flew, flown; sang, sung; wrote, written; drove, driven; blew, blown]

Distribute Blackline Master 52. Explain that the words in the boxes are different forms of five irregular verbs. Read the verbs aloud. Pair students of varying language levels. Read aloud and discuss the directions with students. Guide students to cut out the words in the boxes. Encourage pairs to manipulate the words on their desks and find the verbs that match. Then have them paste the verbs in the correct order in the chart. Have students complete the activity in pairs.

Informal Assessment

Have students turn to page 182, and point to the photo on the page. Ask, *What do you see here? What verb could you use to describe the action in the picture? What are the past and past participle forms of the verb? Is the verb regular or irregular?*

Use the following chart to assess and reteach.

Are students able to:	
orally describe the actions of a picture?	Reteach using Language Support Activity on TE page 184 for oral practice.
identify regualr and irregular verbs?	Reteach using the Language Support Activity on TE page 186.
recognize and name the present, past, and past participle forms of irregular verbs?	Reteach using the Reteach Activity on TE page 187.

Handy Verbs

Look at the pictures. Think about the action in each picture. Cut out each picture.

beat, beat, beaten

throw, threw, thrown

catch, caught, caught

snap, snapped, snapped

strum, strummed, strummed

paint, painted, painted

write, wrote, written

clap, clapped, clapped

Irregular Verb Mix-up

Read the words in the boxes. The boxes contain different forms of irregular verbs in the present, past, and past participle form. Cut out the words. Match the verb forms that go together. Paste the verb forms in their correct positions on the chart.

		Present	Past	Past Participle
1.				
2.				
3.				
4.				
5.				

begin	rung	swim	ate	begun
swam	rang	began	eat	ring
eaten	take	taken	took	swum

It's Highly Irregular

Look at the pictures. Read the verbs. Read the incomplete sentences. Write the past or past participle form of the verb to complete each sentence.

fly	Past: The cat _____ a kite all morning Past Participle: The cat had never _____ a kite before.
sing	Past: The frog _____ in the choir last Thursday. Past Participle: The frog had never _____ in the choir before.
write	Past: Spot _____ a short story this afternoon. Past Participle: Spot had never _____ a short story before.
drive	Past: The bunny _____ to the party last Saturday. Past Participle: The bunny had never _____ to a party before.
blow	Past: The squirrels _____ bubbles yesterday. Past Participle: The squirrels had never _____ bubbles before.

PREFIXES AND SUFFIXES

Introduce this lesson before Pupil Edition pages 202–203.

I. DEVELOP ORAL LANGUAGE
Oral Focus on Vocabulary Skill

Objective: Orally describe pictures and identify how prefixes and suffixes change the meaning of words.

Whole Group Oral Language Activity

Write the word *happy* under a smiling face on the chalkboard. Then draw a picture of a sad face. Ask: *What is another word for sad?* (unhappy) Write it under the sad face. Underline the prefix *un-* and explain that a prefix is a word part that is added to the beginning of a base word to change its meaning. Ask: *What is the base word of unhappy?* (happy) *What is the prefix?* (un-) *What do you think the prefix un- might mean?* (not) Together with the class brainstorm a list of words beginning with the prefix *-un.* Write each word on the chalkboard and invite volunteers to identify the base word and tell how the prefix changes its meaning. Then use *happiness* to teach the suffix *-ness,* meaning *the condition of.*

Scaffolded Verbal Prompting

Use the following verbal prompts to help students better understand prefixes and suffixes and how they change the meaning of a base word.

Nonverbal Prompt for Active Participation

Pre-Production: *Point to the picture of the happy face. Point to the picture of the unhappy face. Now point to the face that is not happy.*

One- or Two-Word Response Prompt

Early Production: *Name the word for the first face. Name the word for the second face.*

Prompt for Short Answers to Higher-Level Thinking Skills

Speech Emergence: *Which picture shows a happy face? Which picture shows an unhappy face? What is the base word of the word* unhappy? *What was added to the word* happy *that changed its meaning?*

Prompt for Detailed Answers to Higher-Level Thinking Skills

Intermediate and Advanced Fluency: *Tell me which face is unhappy. What is the base word of* unhappy? *How does the prefix change the meaning? Name another word with the base word happy.*

II. DEVELOP VOCABULARY SKILLS IN CONTEXT
Visual/Physical Focus on Vocabulary Skill

Objective: Discover new words by adding prefixes and suffixes.

Small Group Activity

Write *prefixes* and *suffixes* on the chalkboard. Introduce two new prefixes, such as *re-* and *in-,* and two new suffixes, such as *-able* and *-ly* and discuss their meanings. Invite volunteers to name words with each prefix and suffix and write the words on the board. Form four small groups of varying language abilities, and assign each group a different prefix or suffix. Ask each group to brainstorm other words.

Partner Activity

Make word cards with suffixes, prefixes, and base words that together form words such as *friend + ly; im + possible;* and *enjoy + able.* Form pairs of varying language levels. Provide each pair with a set of word cards. Have partners work together to separate the prefixes and suffixes from the base words and put them in two separate piles. Tell them one student should select a base word, while the other selects a prefix or suffix. Have the students stand side-by-side and say their word parts aloud to see if they form a word. If they don't, have them switch places and try again. If the parts still do not form a word, have them discard their word part and select a new word part. When partners make a word, have them color each part the same color. Continue until all the parts have been matched.

Technology Link

Provide a list of base words to which a certain prefix or suffix can be added. Invite pairs to use a word processor to type the words, then type them again adding the prefix or suffix to make a new word.

III. PRACTICE VOCABULARY SKILLS
Written Focus on Vocabulary Skill

Objective: Match prefixes or suffixes and base words to form new words.

Materials: Blackline Master 53; scissors, paste

Introduce Blackline Master 53: Create a Word

Form student pairs of varying levels. Distribute Blackline Master 53. Look at the pictures and discuss them with students. Read aloud the directions and complete the first exercise together. Have pairs work together to complete the rest.

Objective: Identify prefixes, suffixes, and base words.

Materials: Blackline Master 54; pencils

Introduce Blackline Master 54: What's the Word?

Distribute Blackline Master 54. Point to each picture and have volunteers describe what is happening in it. Ask volunteers to read aloud each word in the word bank. Read aloud the directions and complete the first exercise together. Have students complete the rest.

Informal Assessment

Have students turn to page 203 in the textbook. Refer them to the second exercise in Practice A. Ask, *What word in the sentence contains a prefix? What is the prefix? What is the base word?* Next, refer them to the fifth exercise in Practice A. Ask, *What word in the sentence contains a suffix? What is the base word? the suffix?*

Use the following chart to assess and reteach.

Are children able to: identify prefixes and suffixes?	Reteach using the Reteach Activity on TE page 203.
use prefixes and suffixes to understand and change word meaning?	Reteach using the Teaching tip on TE page 202.

Create a Word

Cut out the cards at the bottom. Pair the two parts that form each word. Paste the parts together on either side of the plus sign.

1.
unhappy = +

2.
cloudless = +

3.
disagree = +

dis	un	less
 **happy**	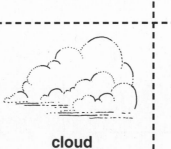 **cloud**	 **agree**

What's the Word?

Read the words in the box. Look at the pictures. Match each word to the picture and write the word on the line. Circle the prefix or suffix and underline the base word.

joyful	quietly
teacher	untied

_____

_____

_____

_____

ORGANIZATION

Introduce this lesson before Pupil Edition pages 204–205.

I. DEVELOP ORAL LANGUAGE
Oral Focus on Composition Skill

Objective: Orally describe a process using spatial descriptions, time-order words, and cause and effect words in order to organize information.

TPR

Whole Group Oral Language Activity

Ask volunteers: *What is in front of you?* (my desk); *What is above your head?* (the ceiling); *What do you see when you look to the left? To the right?* Write the words *in front of, above, left,* and *right* on the chalkboard. Explain that these words are *spatial descriptions*, or words that describe how things are arranged. Invite the class to perform a sequence of three steps: *Stand up, clap your hands, stomp your feet.* Write the words *first, next,* and *then* on the chalkboard. Then invite a volunteer to tell what he or she did in order. Explain that telling things in order and using time-order words such as *first, next, then, before* and *after* are helpful when describing or explaining a process. Words that show cause and effect, such as *because,* are another way to organize a written composition.

Scaffolded Verbal Prompting

Use the following verbal prompts to help students better understand spatial descriptions, time-order words, and cause-effect words.

Nonverbal Prompt for Active Participation

Pre-Production: *Look above you. Look to the left. Look to the right. Now show me what you did last.*

One- or Two-Word Response Prompt

Early Production: *Look up. What is above you? Look to the left. What do you see? Look to the right. Show me what you did first.*

Prompt for Short Answers to Higher-Level Thinking Skills

Speech Emergence: *Where is the ceiling? Where is the floor? What is to your left? What is to your right?*

Prompt for Detailed Answers to Higher-Level Thinking Skills

Intermediate and Advanced Fluency: *Which words tell where things are? Which words tell things in order?*

II. DEVELOP COMPOSITION SKILLS IN CONTEXT
Visual/Physical Focus on Composition Skill

Objective: Give directions using spatial descriptions, time-order words, and cause and effect.

TPR

Small Group Activity

Take the whole class on a walk to the library. Have students think about how to give directions as they walk. When you return, have small groups use time-order and spatial words in their directions.

Technology Link

Type a sequence of three simple steps using time-order words into a word processing program, but arrange them out of order. Have students use the Cut and Paste feature to rearrange the steps.

Extension: Ask students to explain what the effect would be if a student did the opposite of what the directions ask.

Partner Activity

Extension: Ask students to write their description into a paragraph describing the process they demonstrated using time-order words, spatial descriptions, and cause and effect words.

TPR

Brainstorm with the class a list of simple processes with which they are familiar, such as *making a peanut butter and jelly sandwich* or *brushing your teeth*. Write the list on the chalkboard. Pair students of varying language levels and have them choose a process to act out for their partner. Have students guess what their partner is doing. Then have the actor demonstrate the process again while describing it with time-order, spatial, and cause-effect words.

III. PRACTICE COMPOSITION SKILLS
Written Focus on Composition Skill

Introduce Blackline Master 55: What is the Order?

Objective: Use time-order words to describe a sequence.

Materials: Blackline Master 55; pencils, scissors, paste

Tell students that explanatory writing describes how to do something, how something works, or what causes an event to occur. Form student pairs of varying levels. Distribute Blackline Master 55. Discuss the pictures and the steps. Read aloud the activity directions with students. Have partners work together to complete the activity.

Introduce Blackline Master 56: I'll Meet You There!

Objective: Choose time-order words and spatial descriptions to explain directions.

Materials: Blackline Master 56; pencils

Tell students to imagine they are writing directions to meet a friend. Distribute Blackline Master 56. Read aloud the words in the word bank and discuss the pictures. Read the sentence below the first picture and fill in the missing word together. Have students work together in small groups to complete the rest of the sentences.

Informal Assessment

Have students turn to page 205. Refer them to the first exercise in Practice A. Ask: *Which word is used to present a step? What kind of word is it?* Then read the third exercise. Ask: *What word is used to describe what will happen? What kind of word is it?*

Use the following chart to assess and reteach.

Are students able to:	
understand the importance of organizing information logically?	Reteach by allowing pre- and early production students to pantomime or draw their responses.
organize information using time-order words, spatial descriptions, and cause-and-effect words?	Reteach using the Reteach Activity on TE page 205.

Name_____ Date_____

What is the Order?

Cut out each picture. Arrange the pictures in the proper sequence to show what happens *first, next,* and *then.* Paste the pictures in the first row of boxes in correct order. Fill in the time-order words to tell the sequence. Then describe another process by drawing the sequence and labeling it with time-order words. Then give your sequence a title.

How to Plant

1.

_____

2.

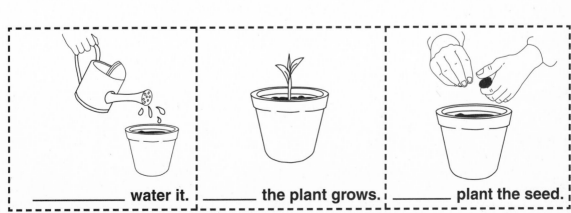

_____ water it. _____ the plant grows. _____ plant the seed.

Name_____ Date_____

I'll Meet You There!

Imagine that you are writing instructions for someone to meet you at a particular location. Look at the pictures. Read the sentences. Fill in the blanks with time-order words or spatial words from the word bank.

left	in front of	right
first	next	then

_____, go down Oak street.

_____, turn _____ on Main Street.

_____ turn _____ just past the fountain.

Meet me _____ the delicatessen.

Introduce this lesson before Pupil Edition pages 210–229.

I. PREWRITE
Oral Warm Up

Objectives: Ask and respond to thoughtful questions. Give precise instructions.

TPR

Whole Group Oral Language Activity

Display illustrations that show simple tasks being performed. Examples could include a person changing a light bulb or a person making a phone call. Ask: *What is the person in this picture doing?* Write responses on the chalkboard. Invite a volunteer to act out one of the processes step-by-step. Have the class discuss the steps.

After students have guessed, have the volunteer explain the process step-by-step, this time using time-order words as they perform. Allow students to ask questions of the volunteer. For example: *What did (Ana) do first? What did (she) do next? What did (she) do last?* Write the words *first, next, then* on the chalkboard and tell students that time-order words such as these are helpful when explaining steps in a process.

Graphic Organizer

Objectives: Choose a topic and find information for an explanatory article.

Materials: Blackline Master 57; pencils

Pre-Production and Early Production

Introduce the Writing Mode

Point out that in explanatory writing, a writer tells how to complete a task or describes a process with step-by-step instructions, using time-order words and spatial descriptions to organize a logical sequence.

Scaffolded Writing Instruction

Using Blackline Master 57, have students draw pictures to show a selection of familiar tasks or processes that can be easily explained. Then they can number and label the pictures.

Speech Emergence

Ask students to number and label their pictures with phrases.

Intermediate and Advanced Fluency

Ask students to list and describe topics for explanatory writing and tell how they would present the ideas to their audience.

Research and Inquiry: Use an Encyclopedia

Have a volunteer name one of the ideas they drew or wrote about in Blackline Master 57. Explain that they might need to find out more about the process in order to explain it more clearly. Model using an encyclopedia to look up the topic. Then have the students work with a partner to look up their topics in an encyclopedia.

II. DRAFT

Objectives:
- Use sequencing strategies to organize ideas.
- Begin drafting a explanatory piece of writing.

Focus on Explanatory Writing

Write the steps for an explanatory piece in the incorrect order on the board and read them aloud. For example: *Put one shoe on each foot. Tie each shoe. Put socks on.* Ask students to tell what should happen first. Invite a volunteer to write number *1* beside it. Then have a volunteer write a number *2* beside the second step, number *3* beside the third step, and so on. Ask a fluent English speaker to explain the process in sequence while other volunteers act it out.

Scaffolded Writing Instruction

Pre-Production and Early Production
Blackline Master 58

Use Blackline Master 58 to help students organize their explanatory article in a logical sequence of steps. Ask them to use drawings to show the sequence in order.

Speech Emergence
Blackline Master 59

Use Blackline Master 59 to assist students in arranging the steps of their processes. They will need to add drawings and short phrases as they explain the steps. Point out that they should use a separate picture or label for each step of the process they explain.

Intermediate and Advanced Fluency

Students may begin to compose an explanatory article. Review the features of explanatory writing before they begin, pointing out that these features need to be a part of their writing. Remind them that their article should be written in a logical sequence with their audience in mind. It should contain clear details that are easy to follow. Ask them to use time-order words and spatial descriptions as they write.

III. REVISE

Objectives:
- Revise an explanatory article.
- Add details to elaborate.

Focus on Elaboration

Write the following sentences on the board and read them aloud with the class:

First get some snow.

Next put ingredients in a bowl.

Then stir it up and eat.

Review the concept of sequence by asking students to point to what happens *first*, *next*, and *then*.

Explain that adding important details helps explain the steps of a process. Have volunteers elaborate on each sentence by adding details that help explain the process. You can ask leading questions such as the following: *What kind of snow do I need to get? What ingredients should I use? How large should the bowl be? How should I mix it together?*

Scaffolded Instruction for Revising

Pre-Production and Early
Production

Blackline Master 58

Speech Emergence

Blackline Master 59

Use students' work in Blackline Master 58 to help them understand the concept of elaboration. Ask them to add more details.

Use students' work in Blackline Master 59 to help them elaborate on their explanatory articles. Ask them to add words and short phrases that show spatial relationships and quantities.

Intermediate and Advanced
Fluency

Students may elaborate on the explanatory article they have started by adding details that help the readers visualize the story.

Technology Link

Have partners type a sequence of steps in a computer and number them. Then have them delete the numbers and replace them with time-order words, adding details and indenting each paragraph.

IV. REVISE • PEER CONFERENCING

Focus on Peer Conferencing

Objectives:
• Participate in peer conferences.
• Give and receive constructive feedback and suggestions for improvement.
• Revise an explanatory article.

Pair pre-production and early-production students with more advanced students to hold peer conferences. Have the more fluent students explain the steps of the process described in the illustrations created by the pre- and early-production students. If paired with another native language speaker, have the pre- and early students explain their process in their native language to the more fluent student as they follow along with the illustrations.

Using page 223 as your guide, prepare a checklist for each proficiency level and write these on the chalkboard, so students may refer to them.

V. PROOFREADING

Focus on English Conventions

Objectives: Demonstrate comprehension of proofreading strategies. Use correct verb tense and check subject-verb agreement.

Say these sentences and ask students what is wrong with them.

First, you must dried the egg. Next, you should painted it.

Review the fact that verbs must be written in the correct tense—*past, present,* or *future.* Ask students what tense the verbs in the sentences show *(past).* Have volunteers correct the sentences.

Next, say these sentences and ask what is wrong with them.

First, I dries the egg. Next, I paints the eggshell.

Review the fact that subjects and verbs must agree. Have volunteers say each sentence using the correct subject-verb agreement.

Ask students to complete Blackline Master 60 for extra practice on the grammar skill, before looking back at their work and checking verb tenses and subject-verb agreement.

After students have completed Blackline Master 60, explain that proofreading includes correcting spelling mistakes. Remind students that some verbs change spelling when the tense changes. Write a list of regular verbs and irregular verbs on the board and review the rules for regular endings. Then explain that there are no set rules in changing irregular verbs. Tell students that if they are in doubt about whether a verb is irregular, or how to change an ending on an irregular verb, they should consult a dictionary. Model, if necessary.

VI. PUBLISH

Objective: Present a neat final copy of an explanatory article and share your work with others.

Using page 226 as a guide, prepare a checklist for each proficiency level and write the list on the chalkboard, so students may refer to them as they prepare the final version of their explanatory article.

Create a Class How-To Book

TPR

Place students in groups of varying language levels. Have the more fluent students read their explanatory articles to the group, acting out steps as necessary. Have others draw pictures to illustrate the steps of the process. For those students who drew illustrations to explain their processes, have them show their illustrations to the group. Then have fluent group members work together to write about the process. Have all the groups bind their articles and illustrations together in one book called *Our Group How-To Book.*

VII. LISTENING, SPEAKING, VIEWING, REPRESENTING

Extension: You might have each group present skits for a mock television show based on their particular how-to book.

Adapt the steps on pages 228–229 to generate activities that will bring out the talents of all students, including those that are in the pre- and early-production stages. Have these students act out steps of a process or help to illustrate an explanatory article.

Informal Assessment

TPR

When assessing students' learning, you need to adapt your expectations of what constitutes an appropriate response. For example, instead of the traditional answers to writing prompts, you may want students to perform an activity that will show how a process is carried out.

Let Me Explain

Think of something you know how to do. Write your topic inside the light bulb. Then make a list of the steps in that process or draw pictures of the steps.

"Ideas for Steps in a Process"

My Topic:

A Step in the Right Direction

Think about a step-by-step process that you find interesting. Draw a picture of each step in the order in which it happens.

1.

2.

3.

4.

5.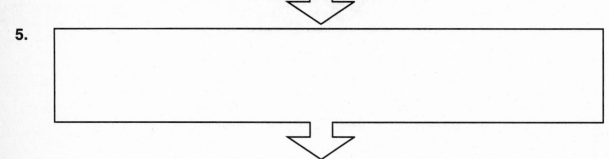

Name_____ Date_____

Step By Step

Think about a step-by-step process that you find interesting. Draw a picture and label each step. Write time-order words that tell when each step happens and spatial directions to help explain what is occurring in each step. Include detailed pictures, phrases, or sentences to help you explain the process.

first/next/then	above/below
before/after	near/next to
left/right	

Verb Tenses and Subject-Verb Agreement

Part A

Read the sentences. Read the underlined verbs. They are written in the present tense. Change the sentences to the past tense by crossing out the verb and writing it in the past tense.

1. First I <u>gather</u> flowers from the garden.

2. Next I <u>find</u> a large vase.

3. I <u>fill</u> the vase with water.

4. Then I <u>arrange</u> the flowers in the vase.

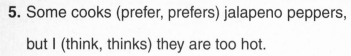

Part B

Read the sentences. Underline the verb that agrees in number with the subject.

1. Many cooks (like, likes) to share their favorite recipes.

2. I (am, is) going to tell you how to make spicy cheese dip.

3. First, you (place, places) eight ounces of cheddar cheese in a large microwavable bowl.

4. Next, you (add, adds) one can of chopped tomatoes and green chilies.

5. Some cooks (prefer, prefers) jalapeno peppers, but I (think, thinks) they are too hot.

6. Then you (heat, heats) the mixture in the microwave oven.

7. I usually (serve, serves) spicy cheese dip with tortilla chips.

I. DEVELOP ORAL LANGUAGE
Oral Focus on Grammar Skill

Objective: Orally describe objects, using adjectives

Whole Group Oral Language Activity

Write the word *Adjective* on the chalkboard. Choose two items that are identical except for the color or size, such as two notebooks. Put them at the back of the classroom, where students can see them. Say: *(Student's name), please bring me the notebook.* Ask the class: *What words could I use to tell which notebook I want?* (green, red, big, little) Write the adjectives that students offer under the word *Adjective.* Then tell the student which notebook you want: *Please bring me the red notebook.* Explain that adjectives are words that tell about nouns and pronouns. They make things clearer.

Write *red notebook* on the board. Ask a student to circle the adjective. (red) Explain that adjectives usually come before the word they tell about, or sometimes they come after a linking verb. Write *The notebook is red* on the board. Have the class identify the verb in this sentence. (is) Then ask a volunteer to circle the adjective. (red) Point out that this adjective comes after the verb.

Explain that adjectives tell *what kind, which one,* and *how many.* Ask students to categorize the adjectives on the board. If necessary, suggest other adjectives so that you have examples from each category.

Scaffolded Verbal Prompting

Use the following verbal prompts to help students better understand adjectives.

Nonverbal Prompt for Active Participation

Pre-Production: *Point to someone wearing a white shirt. Now point to someone wearing a blue shirt. Who is wearing a yellow shirt?*

One- or Two-Word Response Prompt

Early Production: *Look at this object.* (Indicate a book, piece of clothing, or other appropriate item.) *What words tell about it?*

Prompt for Short Answers to Higher-Level Thinking Skills

Speech Emergence: *Look at your shoes and my shoes. How are they different? What adjectives did you use to tell how they are different?*

Prompt for Detailed Answers to Higher-Level Thinking Skills

Intermediate and Advanced Fluency: *Look at the picture on page 257. Describe the tree. What descriptive words did you use? What are these words called?*

II. DEVELOP GRAMMAR SKILLS IN CONTEXT
Visual/Physical Focus on Grammar Skill

Objective: Develop and demonstrate an understanding of adjectives

TPR

Whole Group Activity

Tell students they are going to play a guessing game. You will say, for example: *I see something tall.* They will raise their hands and guess what it is. They must point to the object they think you mean and describe it with the adjective and a noun, such as a *tall bookcase.* When students guess correctly (or offer a response that makes sense), write the adjective and noun on the board. Have a volunteer circle the adjective, and ask another volunteer to draw an arrow from the adjective to the word it describes. Then have students practice giving commands to each other, that contain at least one adjective, such as, *Put a long yellow pencil by the window.*

Small Group Activity

Extension: Have each group describe its picture in a sentence. Write the sentence on the chalkboard. Ask other students to circle the adjectives in the sentence and draw arrows to show which nouns or pronouns they modify.

Give each group art materials and two or three adjectives written on a card, such as *heavy, green, four.* Ask each group to draw a picture that illustrates its adjectives (for example: four large, green dinosaurs). Then have each group share its picture with the class. Ask the class to guess which adjectives the group was trying to show. Also encourage students to name other adjectives that help describe the picture. Create a running list of adjectives on the board.

Partner Activity

Extension: Ask volunteers to read the phrases on the puzzles aloud. Explain that the words written on the puzzles could be the subject of a sentence. Have the pairs add a predicate to each subject to form a complete sentence. Ask each pair to share one of their sentences with the class.

Provide each pair with a copy of Blackline Master 61 and scissors. Read and discuss the instructions. Point out that each puzzle has two parts: a noun, and an adjective that tells about the noun. The picture on each puzzle illustrates the noun and adjective. Ask the partners to cut out the puzzles, turn the pieces upside down and mix them up, and then take turns drawing pairs of pieces until they have matched all the nouns with the appropriate adjectives.

Technology Link

Type the three sentences below into a word processing program. Pair students of different language levels. Have them decide which adjective makes sense in each sentence. Then they can use the delete key or backspace to eliminate the other adjective, along with the parentheses and the comma.

1. I left my (warm, loud) coat at home.
2. I made a sandwich with (wet, two) slices of bread.
3. Let's go into the (shiny, shoe) store.

III. PRACTICE GRAMMAR SKILLS
Written Focus on Grammar Skill

Use Blackline Masters 62 and 63 to reinforce the understanding and use of adjectives in the context of the sentence.

Informal Assessment

Objective: Decide which of two adjectives makes sense in a sentence

Materials: Blackline Master 62; pencils

[**Answers:** 1. deep/valley; 2. hard/rock; 3. Many/canyons; 4. rocky/sides]

Have students turn to page 257 in their textbooks. Read aloud a sentence from More Practice A. Ask: Which words in this sentence are adjectives? What noun or pronoun does each adjective describe?

Introduce Blackline Master 62: Adjectives in a Canyon

Organize the class into pairs of varying language levels. Distribute Blackline Master 62. Read aloud and discuss the directions with students. Encourage pairs to discuss both answer choices before deciding which adjective makes sense in each sentence. Then have the pairs write the adjective they chose on the line and draw an arrow to the word that the adjective describes.

Informal Assessment

Have students turn to pages 257 in their textbooks. Read aloud a sentence from More Practice A. Ask: *Which words in this sentence are adjectives? What noun or pronoun does each adjective describe?*

Introduce Blackline Master 63: Adjectives over a Cliff

Objective: Choose the best adjectives to complete sentences

Materials: Blackline Master 63; pencils

[**Answers:** 1. high/Cliffs; 2. rocky/cliffs; 3. small/pieces; 4. These/pieces; 5. ocean/waves]

Form student pairs and distribute Blackline Master 63. Read aloud and discuss the directions with students. Encourage the pairs to read all the adjectives before deciding which one fits in each sentence. Remind the students to draw a line from each adjective to the sentence it goes with, and then to circle the word in the sentence that the adjective describes.

Informal Assessment

Have students turn to pages 256 and 257, and point to the photograph. Ask: *What do you see here? What adjectives can you use to describe this picture?*

Use the following chart to assess and reteach.

Are students able to:	
identify the adjectives in sentences?	Reteach using the Meeting Individual Needs Reteach page on TE page 257.
identify the noun or pronoun each adjective describes?	Reteach using part B of the Extra Practice page on TE page 324.
choose an adjective that makes sense in a specific context?	Reteach using the Language Support Activity on TE page 256.

Matching Adjectives and Nouns

Cut out the four puzzles. Then cut the puzzle pieces apart on the lines. Turn all the pieces upside down and mix them up. Take turns flipping over two pieces. If the pieces you choose go together, say the noun and adjective together and take the pieces. If they don't go together, turn the pieces upside down again. Continue until all the nouns and adjectives are matched.

striped **fish**	**three** **cars**

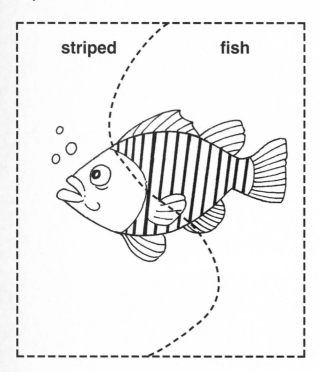
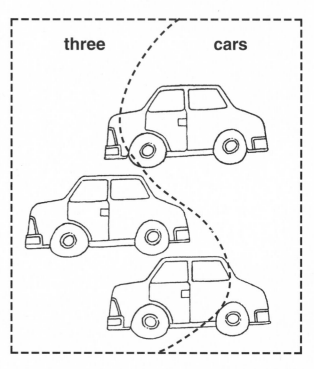

sad **dog**	**sleepy** **child**

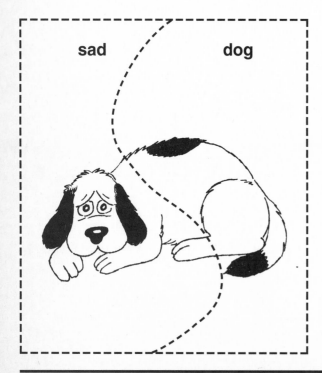
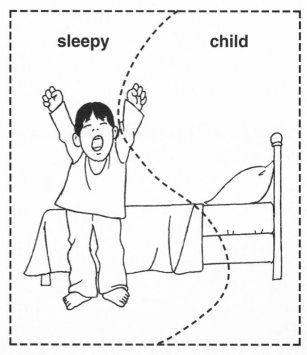

Adjectives in a Canyon

Look at the picture and read the sentences. Decide which adjective fits into each sentence. Write that adjective on the line. Draw an arrow from the adjective to the word it describes.

1. A canyon is a _____ valley.
      four   deep

2. Rivers cut canyons into the _____ rock.
           leafy   hard

3. _____ canyons still have a river at the bottom.
   Many   Bright

4. The sides of a canyon are very _____.
           cheerful   rocky

Adjectives over a Cliff

Read the adjectives and the sentences. Decide which adjectives fits into each sentence. Draw a line from that adjective to its sentence. Circle the word in the sentence that the adjective describes.

sandy   **1.** Cliffs are _____ and rocky.

These   **2.** Waves keep hitting the _____ cliffs.

rocky   **3.** The waves break off _____ pieces of rock.

high   **4.** _____ pieces fall into the ocean.

small   **5.** Waves crush the rock into sand, and form a _____ beach.

COMPARATIVE AND SUPERLATIVE ADJECTIVES

I. DEVELOP ORAL LANGUAGE
Oral Focus on Grammar Skill

Objective: Orally use adjectives to make comparisons

Whole Group Oral Language Activity

Find three items that are identical except for size, such as three pencils of different lengths. Display two of the items and say: *Pretend that you want one of these pencils. How can you tell me which one you want?* Guide students to ask for the longer one. Write *longer* on the chalkboard and underline the *-er* ending. Then add the third pencil to the group. Point to the longest pencil and ask: *How would you ask for this one?* Guide students to use the word *longest* and write it on the board, underlining the *-est.* Repeat the process to show the *shorter* and *shortest* pencils.

TPR

Explain that the students are comparing the pencils, telling how they are the same and different. Ask students to tell how many things they are comparing. Stress that they are to use the *-er* ending to compare two things and *-est* to compare three or more things. Make up TPR commands using the objects students have described. (For example: *Pick up the longest pencil. Point to the biggest desk.*) Have students follow the commands to demonstrate their comprehension of comparative and superlative adjectives.

Scaffolded Verbal Prompting

Use the following verbal prompts to help students make comparisons using adjectives.

Nonverbal Prompt for Active Participation

Pre-Production: *Point to the shortest pencil. Which is the longest one? Now point to something that is bigger than a pencil.* (any object, not just other pencils)

One- or Two-Word Response Prompt

Early Production: *Look at these three pencils. What words can you use to tell them apart?* (long, longer, longest; short, shorter, shortest)

Prompt for Short Answers to Higher-Level Thinking Skills

Speech Emergence: *Look at my hair and your hair. What words tell how they are the same? What words tell how they are different?*

Prompt for Detailed Answers to Higher-Level Thinking Skills

Intermediate and Advanced Fluency: *Look at the pictures on pages 266 and 267. How could you compare the monkey and the elephant? What do we call words that compare or describe*? (adjectives)

II. DEVELOP GRAMMAR SKILLS IN CONTEXT
Visual/Physical Focus on Grammar Skill

Objective: Develop and demonstrate understanding of comparative and superlative adjectives

Materials: Blackline Master 64; scissors (for teacher only)

Whole Group Activity

Make several copies of Blackline Master 64 and cut the pictures apart. Give each student one picture, but distribute only one longest and one shortest pencil, one biggest and one smallest ball, one thickest and one thinnest book, and one tallest and one shortest tree. Give the remaining students medium-sized pictures.

Ask the students with pencil pictures to stand in a line and compare their pictures. Have them decide who has the pictures with the longest and shortest pencils. Ask how many pencils are being compared. Remind them that because they are comparing more than two, they need to use the -est ending. Continue with the other objects.

Small Group Activity

TPR

Extension: Have the members of each group make up a sentence that describes one of their pictures. Write the sentence on the chalkboard. Ask other students to tell what, if anything, is being compared in the sentence. (Remember that the positive form of an adjective, such as young, does not compare anything.)

Give each group art materials and an adjective that can be used for making comparisons, such as *young, warm, cold, mean, fast, slow, short, wide, thin,* or *thick.* Ask each group to draw three pictures that illustrate the three forms of that adjective (for example: *young, younger* and *youngest*). Then have each group share its three pictures with the class. Ask the class to guess which adjective the group was illustrating and to tell the three forms of that adjective.

Partner Activity

Invite the partners to tell each other about the funniest, scariest, or strangest thing they ever saw. Ask them to tell each other why this thing was funnier, scarier, or stranger than anything else they have ever seen. Provide time for several volunteers to share with the class what their partners told them. Ask the class to help you listen for comparative and superlative adjectives. On the chalkboard, keep a running list of the ones you hear.

Technology Link

Help students create a two-column table, with the headings *Comparative* and *Superlative.* Then ask them to type adjectives into their appropriate columns.

III. PRACTICE GRAMMAR SKILLS
Written Focus on Grammar Skill

Use Blackline Masters 65 and 66 to reinforce understanding and use of comparative and superlative adjectives.

Introduce Blackline Master 65: Comparing Kangaroos

Objective: Complete sentences by choosing the correct form of adjectives

Materials: Blackline Master 65; pencils

[**Answers:** 1. smaller; 2. biggest; 3. stronger; 4. largest]

Organize the class into pairs of varying language levels. Distribute Blackline Master 65. Read aloud and discuss the directions with students. Tell the pairs to read all the sentences and look at the picture. Encourage them to discuss both adjective forms for each sentence before choosing one to write on the line.

Informal Assessment

Have students turn to page 267 in their textbooks. Read aloud a sentence from More Practice A. Ask: *Which word in this sentence is an adjective that compares? What is the adjective comparing? How many things does it compare?*

Introduce Blackline Master 66: Comparing Cats

Objective: Form comparative and superlative adjectives to complete sentences

Materials: Blackline Master 66; pencils

[**Answers:** 1. faster; 2. smallest; 3. bigger; 4. loudest]

Form student pairs and distribute Blackline Master 66. Read aloud and discuss the directions with students. Look at the picture together. Point out that lions are cats. Invite students to name other kinds of cats (leopard, tiger, mountain lion, cheetah, lynx, ocelot). Ask volunteers to tell the comparative and superlative forms of the adjective for number 1 (faster, fastest). Then have the pairs complete the activity. Encourage them to decide whether each sentence compares two things—or more than two things—before writing the comparative or superlative form of the adjective on the line.

Informal Assessment

Have students turn to page 266, and point to the photo on the page. Ask: *Would you rather have a monkey or a cat for a pet? Why? What adjectives can you use to compare monkeys and cats as pets?* (cuter, tamer, easier to feed, friendlier)

Use the following chart to assess and reteach.

Are students able to: identify the comparative and superlative adjectives in sentences?	Reteach using part A of the Extra Practice page on TE page 328 for oral practice.
identify which things are being compared?	Reteach using part B of the Extra Practice page on TE page 329.
choose the correct comparative or superlative adjective in a specific context?	Reteach using the Meeting Individual Needs Reteach page on TE page 267.

Comparing Pictures

To the teacher: Make several copies of this page. Cut out the pictures and distribute them to students as described in the lesson.

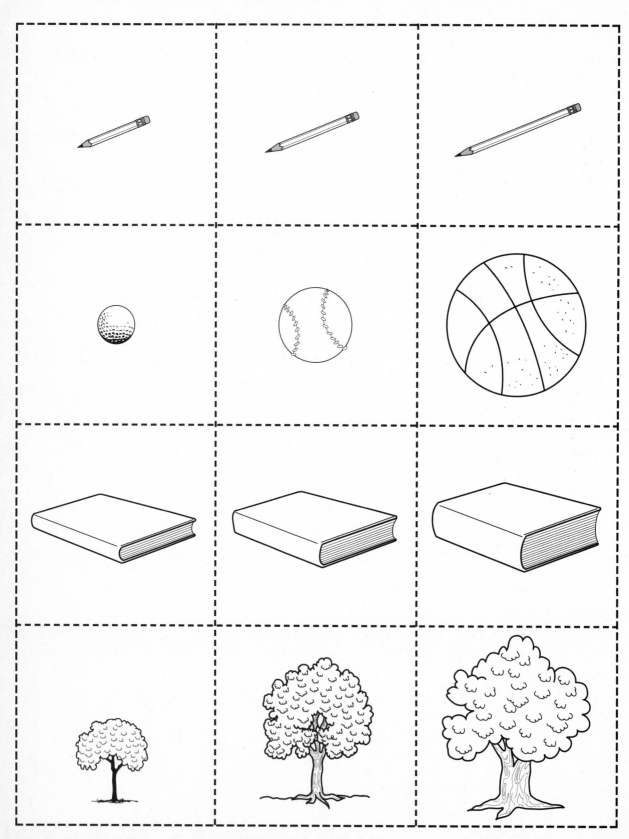

Comparing Kangaroos

Look at the picture and read the sentences. Decide which adjective fits in each sentence. Write the correct adjective on the line.

1. The rat kangaroo is much _____ than the red kangaroo.

                    smaller   smallest

2. The red kangaroo is the _____ of all kangaroos.

                  bigger   biggest

3. A kangaroo's back legs are much _____ than its front legs.

                          stronger   strongest

4. The red kangaroo is the _____ animal that carries its babies in a pocket.

                  larger   largest

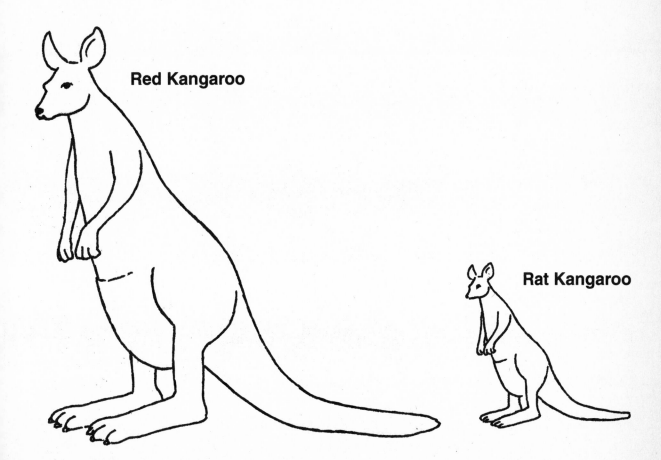

Red Kangaroo

Rat Kangaroo

Comparing Cats

Look at the picture and read the sentences. Decide whether each sentence is comparing two things or more than two things. Change the adjective in parentheses to its comparative or superlative form. Write the correct form on the line.

1. Which of these cats runs _____? (fast)

2. Of all the kinds of cats, which are the _____? (small)

3. The lion's mane makes him look _____ than he is. (big)

4. Lions have the _____ roar I ever heard. (loud)

COMPARING WITH *MORE* AND *MOST*, *GOOD* AND *BAD*

I. DEVELOP ORAL LANGUAGE
Oral Focus on Grammar Skill

Objective: Orally make comparisons using *more* and *most* and the correct forms of *good* and *bad*

Whole Group Oral Language Activity

Have students look at the pictures on pages 266 and 267. Ask: *Which animal is more powerful?* Write *more powerful* in another column. Explain that when we use long adjectives to compare two things, we add the word *more* instead of the ending *-er*. Write *powerfuler* on the board and invite students to try saying this word. Have them notice how hard it is to say. Erase them, explaining that they are not real words.

Return to the two pictures. Ask: *Which animal would make a better pet? Which would make a worse pet?* Write *better* and *worse* in a third column. Explain that the comparative forms of some adjectives are irregular: they aren't formed with *-er* or *more*. For example, *good* becomes *better* and *bad* becomes *worse*.

Point out that students have been comparing just two things, the monkey and the elephant. Have them add in the penguins on page 268. Now ask: *Which of these three kinds of animals is most powerful?* Explain that long adjectives use *most* instead of *-est* when comparing more than two things. *Powerfullest* is not a real word. Ask students to think of other long adjectives that use *more* or *most*.

Scaffolded Verbal Prompting

Use the following verbal prompts to help students better understand and use various forms of comparative and superlative adjectives.

Nonverbal Prompt for Active Participation

Pre-Production: *Look at the animals on pages 266 and 267. Point to the one that is more dangerous. Show me which one is a better climber.*

One- or Two-Word Response Prompt

Early Production: *Look at the animals on pages 266 and 267. What words could you use to compare them?*

Prompt for Short Answers to Higher-Level Thinking Skills

Speech Emergence: *What is the most interesting thing you do every day? What makes this activity more interesting than others?*

Prompt for Detailed Answers to Higher-Level Thinking Skills

Intermediate and Advanced Fluency: *Why do you think some people are more cheerful than others? What makes them more cheerful?*

II. DEVELOP GRAMMAR SKILLS IN CONTEXT
Visual/Physical Focus on Grammar Skill

Objective: Develop and demonstrate understanding of comparisons with *more* and *most, good* and *bad*

Materials: Blackline Master 67; scissors; glue or paste (optional)

TPR

Whole Group Activity

Draw three simple pictures on the chalkboard: an ice-cream cone with one scoop of ice cream, an ice-cream cone with two scoops, and an ice-cream cone with three scoops of ice cream. Say: *Point to the ice-cream cone that looks good, then the one that looks better, and now the one that looks best.* Then direct students to point to the cone that would be *delicious/more delicious/most delicious.* Write the appropriate adjectives under the pictures.

Draw a second set of three pictures on the chalkboard: an empty ice-cream cone with one scoop of ice cream on the ground then one with two scoops on the ground; then one with three scoops on the ground. Say: *Point to the picture that shows something bad, something worse, and the worst situation.* Continue with *disappointing/more disappointing/ the most disappointing.* As before, you might write the appropriate adjectives under the pictures.

TPR

Small Group Activity

Give each group art materials and a long adjective that can be used for making comparisons (for example: *cheerful, difficult, beautiful, wonderful, curious, colorful, terrible, important, surprising, careful, interesting, dangerous, powerful*). Ask each group to draw three pictures that illustrate the positive, comparative, and superlative forms of that adjective (for example: *colorful, more colorful, most colorful*). Then have each group share its three pictures with the class. Ask the class to guess which adjective the group was illustrating.

Partner Activity

Extension: Ask each pair to describe a picture from the worksheet in a sentence using a positive, comparative, or superlative adjective. Write the sentence on the board. Have students identify the adjective and decide whether it is used correctly.

Pair students of different language abilities. Give each pair a copy of Blackline Master 67 and scissors. Read and discuss the directions. Make sure students understand the adjectives for each row of pictures. Give students time to cut out the pictures and arrange them in order, according to the adjectives. If you wish, have them cut out the adjectives and paste them as labels on the appropriate pictures.

Technology Link

Have students type a list of long adjectives, using both *more* and *most.* Show them how to highlight and select *more* and *most.* Then help them select different fonts and colors for each of these words.

III. PRACTICE GRAMMAR SKILLS
Written Focus on Grammar Skill

Use Blackline Masters 68 and 69 to reinforce understanding of comparative and superlative adjectives.

Introduce Blackline Master 68: Comparing with *More* and *Most*

Objective: Complete sentences by choosing the correct forms of comparative and superlative adjectives

Materials: Blackline Master 68; pencils

[Answers: 1. most interesting; 2. bigger, fatter; 3. more skillful; 4. most curious]

Organize the class into pairs of varying language levels. Give each pair a copy of Blackline Master 68. Read aloud and discuss the directions with students. Encourage pairs to discuss both forms of the adjective before underlining the one they think is correct.

Informal Assessment

Have students turn to page 269 in their textbooks. Read aloud a sentence from More Practice A. Ask: *Which form of the adjective is correct in this sentence? How do you know?* (If you wish, repeat this brief exercise with More Practice A on page 271.)

Introduce Blackline Master 69: Comparing with *Good* and *Bad*

Objective: Complete comparative sentences by choosing the correct form of the adjectives *good* and *bad*

Materials: Blackline Master 69; pencils

[Answers: 1. worse; 2. better; 3. worst; 4. better; 5. best; 6. worst]

Form student pairs and distribute Blackline Master 69. Ask students what kind of weather they like best. Discuss the weather shown in the picture. Then read aloud and discuss the directions with students. Encourage the pairs to consider whether each sentence compares two things or more than two things before they underline the adjective they think is correct.

Informal Assessment

Have students turn to pages 270 and 271, and point to the photos. Ask students to name the season shown. (fall) Ask: *Which season do you like best? Which do you think is the worst season? Is any season better than summer? What adjectives have we used to compare the seasons?* (better, best, worse, worst, hottest, sunnier)

Use the following chart to assess and reteach.

Are students able to:	
tell when to use *more* and *most* to form comparative and superlative adjectives?	Reteach using the Meeting Individual Needs Reteach page on TE page 269 for oral practice.
make comparisons with the correct forms of *good* and *bad*?	Reteach using parts A and B of the Extra Practice page on TE page 331.
choose the correct comparative or superlative adjective in a specific context?	Reteach using part C of the Extra Practice pages on TE pages 330 and 331.

Comparing Things

Read the adjectives and cut out the three pictures in each row. Put the picture in order to illustrate the adjectives. Make up a sentence that describes each picture. Use a positive, comparative, or superlative adjective.

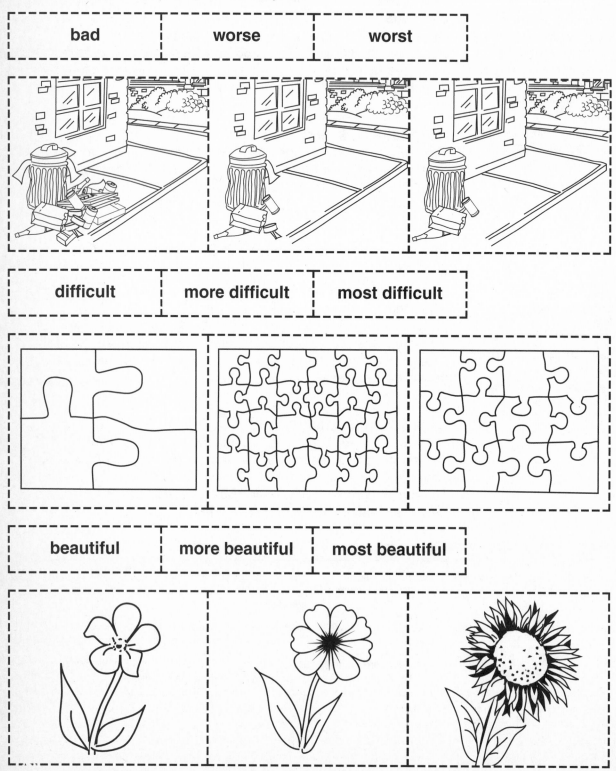

bad	worse	worst
difficult	more difficult	most difficult
beautiful	more beautiful	most beautiful

Comparing with *More* and *Most*

Look at the picture and read the sentence that goes with it. Decide which adjective correctly completes the sentence. Underline the correct adjective.

1. Many people think penguins are the (most interesting, interestingest) birds.

2. Penguins are (more big, bigger) and (more fat, fatter) than most birds.

3. Penguins are (more skillful, skillfuler) at swimming than at flying.

4. Penguins might be the (most curious, curiousest) of all birds.

Comparing with *Good* and *Bad*

Look at the picture and read the sentences. Decide which adjective is correct in each sentence. Underline the correct adjective.

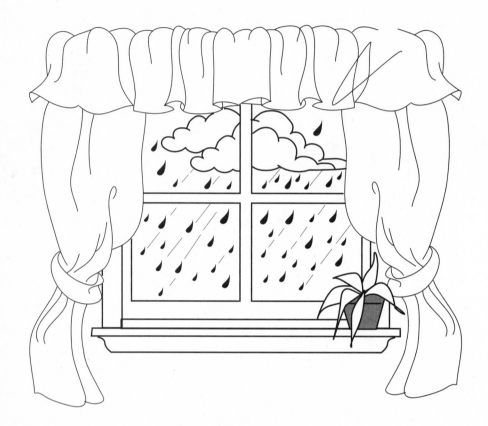

1. The rain is (worse, worst) now than it was this morning.

2. Will the weather be (better, best) tomorrow?

3. I think cold, rainy days are the (worse, worst) of all.

4. Any kind of weather is (better, best) than rain!

5. I like sunny days (better, best) of all.

6. What is the (worse, worst) weather you have ever seen?

SYNONYMS AND ANTONYMS

Introduce this lesson before Pupil Edition pages 288–289.

I. DEVELOP ORAL LANGUAGE
Oral Focus on Vocabulary Skill

Whole Group Oral Language Activity

Objective: Orally describe and recognize words that are synonyms or antonyms

Direct students to page 288 of their textbooks. Ask them to think of words to describe the picture of the pyramids in the desert, such as *tall, hot, sandy.* Write their ideas on the board. Now ask them to think of words that have almost the same meanings, for example, *high, warm, gritty.* Write those in a column labeled *Synonyms.* Explain that synonyms are words that have the same or almost the same meanings. Ask students to think of words that mean the opposite of the words on the board, such as *short, cold, grassy.* Write these in a column labeled *Antonyms.* Tell students that these are words that mean the opposite of each other. Have volunteers come to the board and add words to the list. Then ask the class to think of antonyms or synonyms for the new words.

TPR

Scaffolded Verbal Prompting

Use the following verbal prompts to help students better understand synonyms and antonyms.

Nonverbal Prompt for Active Participation

Pre-Production: *Point to something big. Is that thing also large? Is it small?*

One- or Two-Word Response Prompt

Early Production: *Name a word that means the same as fast. Name a word that means the opposite of fast.*

Prompt for Short Answers to Higher-Level Thinking Skills

Speech Emergence: *Name two words that are synonyms. Name two words that are antonyms.*

Prompt for Detailed Answers to Higher-Level Thinking Skills

Intermediate and Advanced Fluency: *What is a synonym? Give some examples. What is an antonym? Give some examples.*

II. DEVELOP VOCABULARY SKILLS IN CONTEXT
Visual/Physical Focus on Vocabulary Skill

Small Group Activity

Objective: Identify antonyms

TPR

Organize the class into small groups of students with varying language abilities. Give each group an index card with one of the following sets of words on it: *tall/short; exciting/calm; lazy/hard-working; strong/weak; quickly/slowly.* Have each group come to the front of the room. Have half of the group act out the first word and half of the group act out the second word. Have the class try to guess the pair of antonyms. Point out that some of their guesses may be synonyms of the word pair.

Partner Activity

Provide each partner with six index cards and some magazines. Have each partner find pictures and make a pair of cards that show either a synonym or an antonym. Have them place the finished cards face down in a pile. Have partners take turns drawing pairs of cards, then determining whether they are synonyms or antonyms. Continue until all the cards have been taken.

Technology Link

Type a list of descriptive words into the computer. Invite pairs to use the thesaurus function in a word processing program to find synonyms for words and type an example next to each word.

III. PRACTICE VOCABULARY SKILLS
Written Focus on Vocabulary Skill

Objective: Match words with their synonym or antonym.

Materials: Blackline Master 70; scissors; glue

Introduce Blackline Master 70: Same or Opposite?

Distribute Blackline Master 70. Read aloud the directions with students. Have students cut out the boxes at the bottom of the page. Complete the first exercise together as a class. Have groups work together to complete the rest of the page.

Objective: Identify synonyms or antonyms and choose words that correctly complete each sentence

Materials: Blackline Master 71; pencils; dictionaries; thesauri

[**Answers:** 1. sheer, 2. exciting, 3. old, 4. shallow, 5. organized, 6. ripe, 7. shabby, 8. lazy, 9. flimsy, 10. ordinary, 11. incredible, 12. immense]

Introduce Blackline Master 71: Which Word Belongs?

Form student pairs of varying language levels. Distribute Blackline Master 71. Read aloud the activity directions with students. Have students choose the correct synonym from the word box to complete the first sentence and write the word on the line. Have pairs continue working through the sentences to complete the exercises, using the dictionary or thesaurus if necessary to clarify definitions.

Informal Assessment

Have students turn to page 289 in the textbook. Refer them to the second exercise in Practice A. Ask, *What words in the sentence are antonyms? (fertile, barren)* Next, refer them to the eighth exercise in Practice B. Ask, *What is a synonym for* huge? *(Possible answers: large, enormous, gigantic)*

Use the following chart to assess and reteach.

Are students able to: identify antonyms?	Reteach by adapting the Reteach Activity on page 289 so that cards are sorted by antonyms.
identify synonyms?	Reteach by using the Teaching Tip on page 288.

Same or Opposite?

Cut out the boxes at the bottom of the page. Look at the pictures and the words. Find a cut-out box that is the synonym or antonym of the word shown in each exercise. When you have correctly matched all of the words, glue the cut-out boxes in the correct space.

towering

synonym

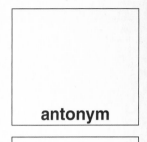

swampy

antonym

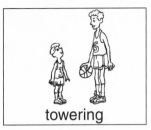

strong

antonym

huge

synonym

fabric

synonym

ancient

antonym

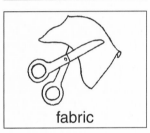

fertile

antonym

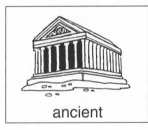

drab

antonym

barren

enormous

tall

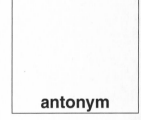

arid

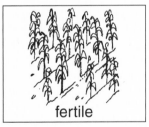

modern

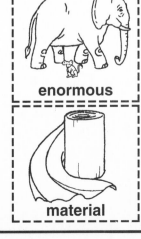

material

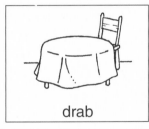

weak

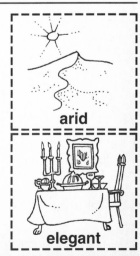

elegant

Which Word Belongs?

Read each sentence. Read the boldface word. Look to see if you are to find a synonym or an antonym for the boldface word. Choose the appropriate synonym or antonym from the word box. Write the correct synonym or antonym on the line.

immense	sheer	ripe	shabby
organized	ordinary	old	flimsy
incredible	lazy	exciting	shallow

1. I could see someone watching from behind the **thin** curtains. (synonym)

_____

2. It was very **calming** to watch the end of the close race. (antonym) _____

3. The pages of the **ancient** book were yellow and brittle. (synonym) _____

4. The water pooled in **deep** ditches. (antonym) _____

5. Jill was very **prepared** to give her report with pictures and notecards. (synonym)

_____

6. The **green** fruit was placed on the shelf. (antonym) _____

7. The dusty, old store was very **elegant** on the inside. (antonym) _____

8. Ants are hard-working insects and are not **industrious.** (antonym) _____

9. The kite was **massive** and fell apart in the strong wind. (antonym) _____

10. It was a very **unique** day with no special events. (antonym) _____

11. Juan could not believe his **amazing** good luck. (synonym) _____

12. The mountain was so **large** Lee wondered if they would ever reach the top.

(synonym) _____

Introduce this lesson before Pupil Edition pages 290–291.

I. DEVELOP ORAL LANGUAGE
Oral Focus on Composition Skill

Objective: Orally describe a picture using sensory details and vivid words

TPR

Whole Group Oral Language Activity

Direct students' attention to the photograph on page 294. Ask, *What do you imagine these astronauts are experiencing?* Write each item on the chalkboard under an appropriate heading for the five senses plus feelings. For example: *dark (sight), footsteps (hearing), rocky (touch), sweet (taste), dust (smell), nervous (feeling).*

Explain that describing a person, place or thing with sensory words helps the reader get a better picture in their mind. Write the following sentences on the board: *The wind blew over the top of the hills. The cold blast of wind whistled over the craggy hills.*

Ask students which sentence gives more details. Have them tell you the sensory words they hear.

Scaffolded Verbal Prompting

Use the following verbal prompts to help students make descriptions more vivid.

Nonverbal Prompt for Active Participation

Pre-Production: *Look at the picture. Imagine you were in the picture. Show me what you would be seeing, hearing, touching, tasting, smelling, and feeling.*

One- or Two-Word Response Prompt

Early Production: *Describe one thing in the picture. Tell me how it would smell, sound, or feel.*

Prompt for Short Answers to Higher-Level Thinking Skills

Speech Emergence: *What are the most interesting parts of the picture? How would you describe those to someone?*

Prompt for Detailed Answers to Higher-Level Thinking Skills

Intermediate Fluency: *Look at the picture. How would you describe the picture to someone else?*

II. DEVELOP COMPOSITION SKILLS IN CONTEXT
Visual/Physical Focus on Composition Skill

Objective: Act out words that describe

TPR

Small Group Activity

Have one member of the group pantomime a noun, for example *dog*. The remaining members will pantomime words that can be used to describe this noun, for example: *lazy, running, furry, happy, disobedient.* Groups take turns coming to the front of the room and pantomiming their noun and descriptive words while the class guesses the noun.

Partner Activity

Extension: Ask pairs to write a paragraph using the picture and including many vivid descriptive details and sensory words. Encourage them to consider the order of their details as they write.

Cut out magazine pictures that have lots of details, one picture for every two students. Have the pair list three vivid descriptive details they see in the picture and three descriptions that have nothing to do with the picture. Have them transfer each of these six items onto index cards. Invite each pair to display its picture and quiz the group, by asking for a show of hands each time a description is read aloud of something actually in the picture.

Technology Link

Encourage students to use the thesaurus feature of a word processing program to find synonyms.

III. PRACTICE COMPOSITION SKILLS
Written Focus on Composition Skill

Introduce Blackline Master 72: Describe It

Objective: Match vivid descriptions with illustrations

Materials: Blackline Master 72; scissors; glue

Form student pairs of varying levels. Distribute Blackline Master 72. Review descriptive details. Read aloud the activity directions with students. Then discuss and complete the first description box together. Have partners work together to complete the rest of the activity.

Introduce Blackline Master 73: Determining Descriptions

Objective: Determine which descriptions match an illustration.

Materials: Blackline Master 73; pencils

Organize the class into small groups of varying abilities. Distribute Blackline Master 73. Review descriptive details. Read aloud the directions with students. Then read through all of the sentences below the illustration to check comprehension. Complete the first exercise together. Have students work together in small groups to complete the rest of the page.

Informal Assessment

Have students turn to page 291. Refer them to number 9 in Practice B. Ask: *What descriptive phrase would fit a kite? What would you see? Hear? Touch? What scents would you smell? Would you taste anything? How would you feel?*

Use the following chart to assess and reteach.

Are students able to:	Reteach by using the Language Support Activity on TE page 290.
choose descriptive words to describe an object?	Reteach by using the Language Support Activity on TE page 290.
construct a descriptive phrase or sentence?	Reteach by using the Reteach Activity on TE page 291.

Describe It

Cut the descriptive phrases from the bottom of the page. Match the descriptive phrase with the part of the picture it describes. When you have matched the phrases with the correct places, glue the descriptions into place.

noisy, squawking bird	tall, leafy tree
heavy, dark raincloud	massive, snow-capped mountains
still, quiet pool of water	crashing, swirling waterfall
broad, grassy plain	cold, snowy field
dry, arid desert	bright, shining sun

Determining Descriptions?

Look carefully at the picture at the top of the page. Read each sentence underneath the picture. If the sentence does NOT describe something in the picture, draw a line through the sentence. If the sentence describes something in the picture, circle the sentence. Go back and look at the circled sentences. Add a descriptive word or phrase in each blank.

1. A man is feeding the _____ pigeons and squirrels.

2. There are _____ clouds in the sky.

3. A girl is flying a _____ kite.

4. The _____ dog is running through the park.

5. The boy is playing in the water in the _____ fountain.

6. The _____ cat is sitting under the tree.

7. A _____ boy is roller-skating.

8. Flying in the air is a _____ bird.

9. A girl is riding a _____ bicycle.

10. In the park, there is a _____ tree.

EXPOSITORY WRITING

Introduce this lesson before Pupil Edition pages 294–315.

I. PREWRITE
Oral Warm Up

Objectives:
• Summarize major ideas
• Relate observations or recollections about a topic

Whole Group Oral Language Activity

Make copies of a picture related to a topic the class has recently studied. For example, give students a diagram of the circulatory system from health class. Put a title, such as Circulatory System, on the board. Have them brainstorm as much information as they can remember about the topic and write their responses on the chalkboard under the title. Have volunteers ask questions about the subject. For example: *What organs make up this system? What is the function of blood?* Explain that the title will be part of the main idea for the writing. Have the students group similar details and questions together.

Introduce the Writing Mode

Graphic Organizer

Objectives:
• Begin prewriting for expository writing
• Use a graphic organizer to record ideas

Explain that expository writing gives information. Using the main ideas and details organized on the board, model a piece of expository writing. *(Example: The main organ of the circulatory system is the heart. Its four chambers help to pump blood throughout the body. The blood supplies the body with oxygen.*

Scaffolded Writing Instruction

Pre-Production and Early Production

Blackline Master 74

Using Blackline Master 74, have students write their topic on the top line. Ask them to draw pictures showing the details they already know about their topic in the top box. In the lower box, ask them to draw pictures showing what they still need to find out about their topic.

Speech Emergence

Ask students to label their pictures and form questions with words or phrases, perhaps using vocabulary related to their chosen subject.

Intermediate and Advanced Fluency

Ask students to write a sentence stating the main idea of their expository writing. Ask them to write phrases and sentences about the details of their topic, and in the lower box, have them place questions they have about their subject.

Research and Inquiry: Use a Card Catalog

Tell students that the card catalogue in a library can help them find books about their topics. Explain that in a computerized card catalogue, you type in your topic, and the computer will give you some choices to look at further. Ask, *Do you know how the cards are arranged in a regular card catalogue?* (alphabetical order) Ask, *Do you know the three types of cards in a regular card catalogue?* (author, subject, title)

II. DRAFT

Objectives:
- Use main idea and details to organize ideas
- Begin drafting a piece of expository writing

Focus on Expository Writing

Model the process of outlining the main idea and details. Write the following ideas for expository writing on the board and read them aloud: *Glaciers change the earth underneath them as they slowly move. Valleys are carved into U shapes by the dirt and rocks pushed along the underside of the glacier. In some places, you can see where glaciers have been in the past because of deep grooves carved into rock.* Ask students to identify the main idea. Then have students identify the details. Have students act out the main idea and details.

Scaffolded Writing Instruction

TPR

Pre-Production and Early Production

Blackline Master 75: Supporting the Main Idea

Speech Emergence

Blackline Master 76: Main Idea and Details

Use Blackline Master 75 to help students organize their expository writing by stating a main idea and supporting it with details. Ask them to use drawings or pictures to show those parts of their expository writing.

Use Blackline Master 76 to assist students in composing their expository writing. They will need to add pictures or drawings and short phrases to express three main ideas related to their topic and supporting details under each one.

Intermediate and Advanced Fluency

Students may begin to compose a piece of expository writing. Review the features of expository writing. Remind them to focus on one main idea per paragraph and several details that support that main idea. Encourage them to use transition words when moving from one main idea to the next.

III. REVISE

Objectives:
- Revise expository writing
- Add transition words to elaborate

Focus on Elaboration

Write the following sentences on the board and read them aloud to the class:

> *Although your heart is only the size of your fist, it is a powerful pump. A glacier moves slowly, yet it has the power to carve a valley.*

TPR

Explain that transitional words such as *although* and *yet* help to connect clauses and make the sentence read more smoothly. Give groups an index card with one of the following words or phrases on it: *after, although, as a result, however, in the first place, instead, similarly, therefore, though, unlike, when,* or *yet.* Ask students to think of sentences using their transition word.

Scaffolded Instruction for Revising

Pre-Production and Early Production

Blackline Master 75: Supporting the Main Idea

Use students' work in Blackline Master 75 to help them understand the concept of transition words. Ask them to draw arrows between the details in the order that they would present them in their expository writing.

Speech Emergence

Blackline Master 76: Main Idea and Details

Use students' work on Blackline Master 76 to help them elaborate on their expository writing. Ask them to add transition words between the detail boxes to show how their expository writing would flow.

Intermediate and Advanced Fluency

Students may elaborate on the expository writing they have started by adding transition words within their paragraphs that help the text flow in a logical sequence.

Technology Link

Have students type their expository writing into a computer. Then have them insert transition words and phrases into their text. Ask them to read their expository writing aloud to a partner to check that their writing flows from one idea to the next.

IV. REVISE • PEER CONFERENCING

Focus on Peer Conferencing

Objectives:
• Participate in peer conferences
• Give and receive constructive feedback and suggestions for improvement
• Revise a piece of expository writing

Partner pre-production and early-production students with more advanced students to hold peer conferences. Have the more fluent students retell the facts they see in the illustrations created by the pre- and early-production students. Encourage the more fluent student to assist with English vocabulary words to add to the expository writing.

Using page 309 as your guide, prepare a checklist for each proficiency level and write these on the chalkboard, so students may refer to them as they engage in a conference.

V. PROOFREADING

Focus on English Conventions

Objectives:
• Demonstrate comprehension of proofreading strategies
• Use comparative and superlative adjectives correctly

Say these sentences and ask what is wrong with them.

I had the goodest time at your party.

My cold couldn't get much badder.

Review the irregular comparative and superlative forms of *good* and *bad—better*, *best* and *worse*, *worst*. Ask students what is wrong in the first sentence (goodest *should be* best). Then ask what is wrong in the second sentence (badder *should be* worse). Explain that proofreading means looking for mistakes in a written work and correcting them.

Objective: Use the correct forms of the adjectives *good* and *bad*

Materials: Blackline Master 77, pencils

Answers:
1. good 2. worst 3. best
4. worse 5. better 6. good
7. worse 8. better 9. best
10. bad

Spelling Tip: Have students keep a topic list with new vocabulary they encounter about that particular topic. They and other students can use this list when they go to write about that topic.

Ask students to complete Blackline Master 77 for extra practice on the grammar skill, before looking back at their work and identifying which phrases might have incorrect forms of the adjectives *good* and *bad*.

After students have completed Blackline Master 77, explain that proofreading includes correcting spelling mistakes. Often when writing expository text, students come across new vocabulary that may be difficult to spell. When they encounter a new word in their research, have them jot down the page number and source in the margin by the word on their draft, so they can easily go back and check their spelling.

Also, model the use of a dictionary by assisting a student in looking up a word. Based on the student's English language ability, have them find the first letter of the word and sound out what they believe will be the second and third letters of the word.

VI. PUBLISH

Objective:
• Present a neat, final copy of expository writing and actively view the work of others

Extension: You might have each group present the material of the more fluent students to the entire class by having the fluent students read their writing while the other students act it out.

TPR

Using page 312 as your guide, prepare a checklist for each proficiency level and write these on the chalkboard, so students may refer to them as they prepare the final version of their expository writing.

Create and Present a Bulletin Board Display
Place students in mixed language-level groups of 4 to 6 students. Have the more fluent students with written texts read their expository writing to the group. Have students who used illustrations for their expository writing show their illustrations to the group. Other group members may then write a caption for the illustration that tells what they see in the picture. Arrange the student writing and illustrations by grouping them according to subject area on a bulletin board entitled, *Learn Something New.*

VII. LISTENING, SPEAKING, VIEWING, REPRESENTING

Adapt the steps on pages 314–315 to generate activities that will bring out the talents of all students, including those that are in the pre- and early-production stages. Have these students act out events or help to illustrate a written work.

Informal Assessment
In all students' work, whether written or illustrated, look to see if they have shown a main idea with details that support that main idea. Look for how well illustrations or text convey the information about the topic to the reader.

Research Your Topic

Draw or write your topic idea on the top line. Draw or write details about what you already know in the top box. Draw or write questions about your topic that you would like to research.

Topic: _____

What do I know?

What do I want to find out?

Supporting the Main Idea

Write or draw the main idea for your expository writing. On each column, support your main idea by drawing details. Place similar details on the same column.

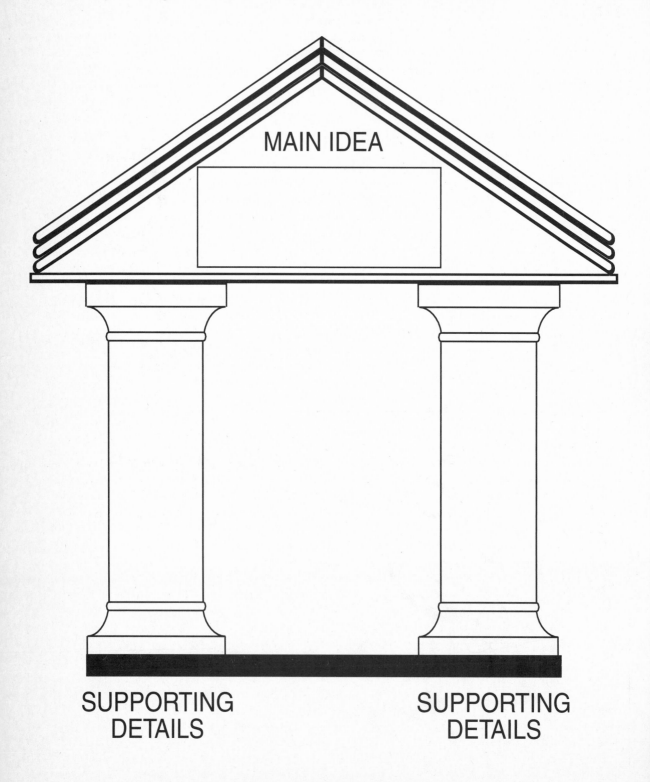

Main Idea and Details

Write your topic at the top of the page. Draw or write a main idea in each box. Put supporting details that go with each main idea in the circles below it.

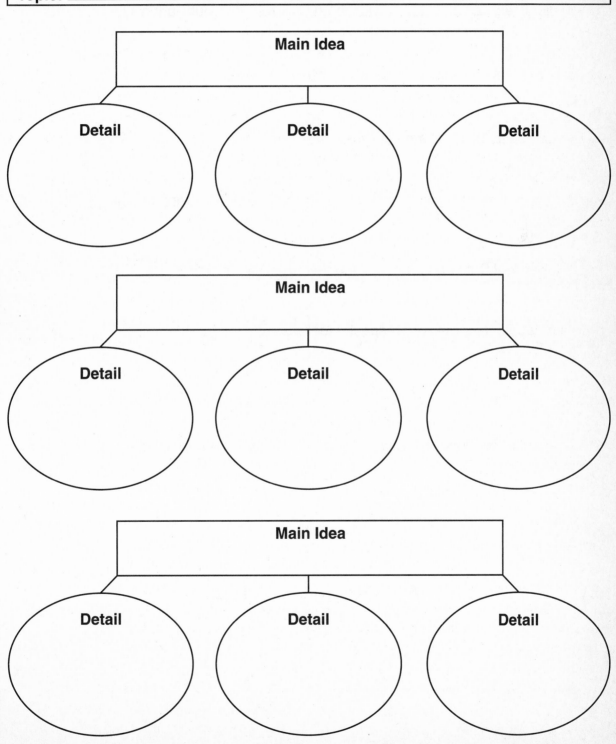

Topic: _____

Main Idea

Detail

Detail

Detail

Main Idea

Detail

Detail

Detail

Main Idea

Detail

Detail

Detail

Choose the Best Word

Read each sentence. Decide which word—*good, better, best, bad, worse, worst*—belongs in the blank. Write the correct word on the line.

1. You did a very _____ job on your report about Sudan.

2. Yuck! That was the _____ flavor I ever tasted.

3. The _____ athlete wins the gold medal.

4. If your behavior is _____ than yesterday, you will be detained.

5. The more you practice, the _____ you will get.

6. When people treat me with respect, I feel _____.

7. If I don't study, I will do _____ on the test than if I do.

8. The clouds are supposed to go away and the weather will get _____ for our softball game.

9. My _____ friend is honest with me.

10. The _____ dog chewed up my tennis shoes.

I. DEVELOP ORAL LANGUAGE
Oral Focus on Grammar Skill

Objective: Orally describe pictures using sentences with personal pronouns and their referents.

Whole Group Oral Language Activity

Ask students to look at the painting on page 374. Ask: *What are these people doing?* (They are running a race.) Write the answer on the chalkboard. Then ask students to point to the front runner. Ask: *What color is the man in front wearing?* (He is wearing blue.) Write that sentence on the board as well. Explain that the referent, or antecedent, of a pronoun is the word or group of words to which the pronoun refers. *People* and *man* are the referents of *they* and *he.* Point out that singular pronouns refer to singular nouns, while plural pronouns refer to plural nouns.

Introduce the theme of meeting challenges by asking what goals the people on pages 374 and 375 might have. Ask students to draw pictures that show a goal they want to achieve. Have them show their pictures and describe their goals in one or two sentences. Encourage them to use personal pronouns (especially *I* and *we*) in their sentences.

Scaffolded Verbal Prompting

Use the following verbal prompts to help students better understand pronouns and referents.

Nonverbal Prompt for Active Participation

Pre-Production: *Look at the picture on page 374 and listen to this sentence:* He is wearing red. *Point to the part of the picture that shows who is wearing red.*

One- or Two-Word Response Prompt

Early Production: *Look at the picture of page 347. Who is winning the race? Use a pronoun in your answer and point to the person you're talking about.*

Prompt for Short Answers to Higher-Level Thinking Skills

Speech Emergence: *Describe one of the people pictured on page 375. What word(s) did you use to tell which person you're talking about? What pronoun did you use?*

Prompt for Detailed Answers to Higher-Level Thinking Skills

Intermediate and Advanced Fluency: *Look at the pictures on pages 374 and 375. In one or two sentences, describe the challenges these people are facing. What pronouns did you use in your sentences? What are the referents for those pronouns?*

II. DEVELOP GRAMMAR SKILLS IN CONTEXT
Visual/Physical Focus on Grammar Skill

Objective: Develop and demonstrate understanding of pronouns and referents.

Materials: Blackline Master 78; scissors; red and blue crayons

Whole Group Activity

Write sentences on the board that describe meeting a challenge, such as: *Carlos is running because Carlos is late for school.* Read the sentence aloud. Ask students if anything sounds odd about them. Elicit the fact that pronouns could be used to avoid repeating the noun *Carlos.* Ask: *Is Carlos a singular noun or a plural noun?* (singular) Let student volunteers erase the repeated noun and write in the appropriate pronoun (*he*). Review the fact that singular referents need singular pronouns while plural referents need plural pronouns.

Circle the words *he is* in the sentence and write *he's* above them. Point out that *he's* is a contraction, a combination of a pronoun and a verb. Explain that contractions are sometimes used in informal writing and speaking. Ask students to think of other pronoun-verb contractions such as *I'm, you're, she's, it's, we're,* and *they're.*

Write more sentences following this pattern on the board. Distribute Blackline Master 78. Have students cut out the pronoun cards and put them in two groups: singular and plural pronouns. Ask the students to clarify all the pronouns as singular or plural, then to color their singular pronoun cards red and their plural pronoun cards blue. Read the sentences on the board. Tell the students to listen and then hold up a card to show which personal pronoun could be used to replace a noun referent in each sentence. Let a student write in the appropriate pronoun, then tell whether it is singular or plural.

TPR

Extension: Make a list of commands based on the students' sentences (for example, *Practice the violin.*). State each command, demonstrating the action for the class. Then let the group members give each other commands to follow. Students should take turns giving commands until each one has had a chance to be the leader.

Small Group Activity

Have each student make up a short sentence that tells how they faced a personal challenge. *(I practiced the violin for an hour every day.)* Instruct the group members to sit in a circle and, one at a time, read their sentences. The other group members must listen and then repeat the sentence, substituting appropriate pronouns or noun/noun phrase referents for the pronoun *I* (for example, *She/You/Mary practiced the violin for an hour every day*).

Partner Activity

Extension: Let volunteers complete the sentences on the board by taping the correct pronoun card in each blank. Ask other students to draw an arrow from each pronoun to its referent.

Write on the chalkboard five or six sentences that describe how people in the news or in history faced a particular challenge. Each sentence should contain a blank to be filled in with a pronoun. (Example: Christopher Columbus believed _____ could find a new way to get to China.)

Technology Link

Type a list of nouns into a word processing program. Have partners think of a pronoun that could replace each noun referent and type it next to the word. Then have them italicize the pronoun.

III. PRACTICE GRAMMAR SKILLS
Written Focus on Grammar Skill

Use Blackline Masters 79 and 80 to reinforce understanding of pronouns and identification of their referents.

Introduce Blackline Master 79: Matching Pronoun Referents

Objective: Identify the referents for pronouns in text and pictures.

Materials: Blackline Master 79; pencils

[**Answers:** we–picture of boys; her–picture of girl She–picture of girl we–picture of boys they–picture of team us–picture of boys we–picture of boys them–picture of team]

Divide the class into pairs of varying levels. Distribute Blackline Master 79. Have a student volunteer read the directions aloud. Discuss the directions with the class. Ask students to point to the underlined pronouns in the first sentence. Ask: *What words do we stand for?* (Christopher and I) Have students find the picture that shows "Christopher and I." Tell them to draw a line from the underlined pronoun *we* to that picture. Then have the pairs complete the activity. Make sure they understand that several pronouns may refer to the same picture.

Informal Assessment

Have students turn to page 339 in their textbooks. Read aloud a sentence from More Practice A. Ask students to identify the pronoun and its referent.

Introduce Blackline Master 80: Circle the Correct Pronoun

Objective: Choose appropriate pronouns to complete sentences.

Materials: Blackline Master 80; pencils

[**Answers:** they; he; she; us; them]

Form student pairs. Distribute Blackline Master 80. Ask students to point to each person in the picture and tell what pronouns could be used to talk about that person. Indicate the boy and girl together and ask: *What pronouns could tell about these children?* (they, them) Ask students to tell whether each pronoun is singular or plural. Read the directions aloud and complete the first sentence together. Ask pairs to complete the remaining sentences by circling the correct pronouns.

Informal Assessment

Have students turn to page 374, and point to the painting. Ask, *Whom do you see in this picture? What pronouns could you use to tell about these people? What is the referent for each pronoun?*

Use the following chart to assess and reteach.

Are students able to:	
identify nouns and pronouns that agree in number and gender?	Reteach using Language Support Activity on TE page 336 for oral practice.
match pronouns with their referents?	Reteach using the Language Support Activity on TE page 338.
replace nouns and noun phrases with appropriate pronouns?	Reteach using the Reteach Activity on TE page 339.

Choosing a Pronoun Referent

Cut out the pronoun cards. Decide whether each pronoun is singular or plural. Color the singular pronoun cards red and the plural pronoun cards blue.

I	he	you
her	them	me
we	she	they
him	us	you

Matching Pronoun Referents

Read each sentence. Look at the underlined pronouns. Find the referent for each pronoun. Draw a line from each pronoun to the picture of its referent.

1. Christopher and I coached Ella's team.

  <u>We</u> gave her a baseball and a bat.

2. <u>She</u> was glad that <u>we</u> were her coaches.

3. The players all had fun, and <u>they</u> won

  the championship.

4. At the end of the season, the players

  gave <u>us</u> a trophy, and we took <u>them</u> out

  for pizza.

Circle the Correct Pronoun

Read the sentences and look at the picture. Read the pronouns underneath each sentence. Decide which pronoun fits in each sentence. Circle it.

1. Nadia and Juan were lost in the city, so _____ looked for a police officer.

    he   they

2. Juan was too shy to ask for help because _____ spoke little English.

    he   we

3. Nadia felt shy too, but _____ knew a police officer would help them get home.

    she   you

4. Nadia said to the police officer, "Please help _____. We're lost. Where is Pine Street?

    him   us

5. The police officer showed _____ the way home.

    me   them

I. DEVELOP ORAL LANGUAGE
Oral Focus on Grammar Skill

Objective: Orally describe photographs using subject and object pronouns.

Whole Group Oral Language Activity

Ask students to look at the photographs on pages 368 and 369. Ask: *What is the woman doing?* (She is climbing a mountain.) *What is the man doing?* (He is taking pictures of her.) Write the answers on the chalkboard. Ask: *Who is doing something?* (she) Point out that the word *she* is the subject of the sentence. It is taking the place of a noun phrase *(the woman on the rope).*

Next, repeat the sentence *He is taking pictures of her.* Ask students to identify the pronouns in that sentence *(he, her).* Ask: *What is the subject of this sentence?* (he) *What is* her? (an object pronoun; the object of the preposition *of).* Explain that object pronouns are used as the object of a verb or as the object of a preposition, such as *at, of, in,* or *to.* Point out the list of subject and object pronouns on PE page 340.

Ask volunteers to make up more simple sentences about the pictures on pages 368 and 369. Tell them not to use pronouns. Then ask other students to replace the subject and/or object of each sentence with an appropriate pronoun.

Scaffolded Verbal Prompting

Use the following verbal prompts to help students better understand subject and object pronouns.

Nonverbal Prompt for Active Participation

Pre-Production: *Look at the pictures on pages 368 and 369. Listen to this sentence:* He is taking pictures of her. *Point to show me who* he *is. Now point to show who we mean by* her.

One- or Two-Word Response Prompt

Early Production: *Look at the pictures on pages 368 and 369. Who is climbing the mountain? Who is taking pictures of her?*

Prompt for Short Answers to Higher-Level Thinking Skills

Speech Emergence: *Tell me about the people on pages 368 and 369. What are they doing?*

Prompt for Detailed Answers to Higher-Level Thinking Skills

Intermediate and Advanced Fluency: *Describe the challenges the people are facing in the photographs on pages 368 and 369. What subject pronouns did you use in your sentences? What object pronouns did you use?*

II. DEVELOP GRAMMAR SKILLS IN CONTEXT
Visual/Physical Focus on Grammar Skill

Objective: Develop and demonstrate understanding of subject and object pronouns.

Materials: Blackline Master 81; scissors; crayons

Whole Group Activity

Talk about ways of solving a problem. Ask: *What do you do when you don't understand your homework? Do you ask a friend or family member for help? Do you wait and ask the teacher the next day?*

Write responses on the board that include subject and object pronouns. Give each student a copy of Blackline Master 81. Have the students cut out the cards and color the subject pronoun card red and the object pronoun card blue. Then read the sentences from the board one at a time. Tell the students to hold up the red card when they hear a subject pronoun and the blue card when they hear an object pronoun.

Small Group Activity

Extension: Have a volunteer from each group read the group's story to the class. The rest of the class students should listen carefully and hold up their subject and object pronoun cards when they hear subject and object pronouns. The group members who are not reading can watch the class to see if everyone holds up the correct cards.

Divide the class into groups. Ask each group to write a language experience story about a recent class field trip, project, or other activity. Give a native English speaker in each group a large sheet of paper and a marker to record the story as the group members tell it. *(Last week our class went to the zoo. We saw a lot of animals. Some of them were sleeping. The penguins were wide awake. They were jumping in the water and swimming around. We watched them for a long time.)* When the group has finished writing its story, the members should underline all the pronouns they used and label each one *S* for subject or *O* for object.

Partner Activity

TPR

Have the partners draw pictures to illustrate the object pronouns *him, her, it,* and *them.* (Or let the students look through old magazines for appropriate pictures to cut out.) Give each pair a few buttons or other markers. Then instruct the partners to take turns telling each other where to put the buttons. (For example, one student might point to a picture of a girl and say "Give a button to her." The other student would then lay a button on the picture of the girl.) Point out that the partners can give buttons to each other ("Give the red button to me") and can move buttons from one person to another ("Take the white buttons from him. Give them to us.") Move around the room listening to the pairs' directions and offering suggestions as needed.

Technology Link

Type the three sentences below into a word processing program. Pair students of varying language levels. Have students retype the sentences using pronouns in place of the underlined nouns and noun phases.

Jean-Claude baked some cookies for his grandmother.

Mrs. Moreau tasted the cookies right away.

"The cookies are delicious," Mrs. Moreau said to Jean-Claude.

III. PRACTICE GRAMMAR SKILLS
Written Focus on Grammar Skill

Use Blackline Masters 82 and 83 to teach understanding, identification, and use of subject and object pronouns.

Objective: Identify and illustrate subject and object pronouns.

Materials: Blackline Master 82; pencils

[**Answers:** 1. subject pronoun–I, object pronoun–me;
2. subject pronoun–I, object pronoun–me;
3. subject pronoun–She, object pronoun–me;
4. subject pronoun–we, object pronoun–us;
5. subject pronoun–I, object pronoun–them]

Introduce Blackline Master 82: Pronouns and Pictures

Distribute Blackline Master 82. Discuss the directions and complete the first item with the class. Tell the students to look at the picture, and have a volunteer read the sentence beneath it. Ask: *What is the subject pronoun?* (I) *What is the object pronoun?* (me) Model how to write *I* and *me* on the correct lines below the sentence. Have students point to the picture of the referent for each pronoun (the sad boy). Then have partners complete the activity together. Remind them to draw a picture that illustrates each sentence.

Informal Assessment

Have students turn to page 341 in their textbooks. Read aloud a few sentences from More Practice A. Ask students to identify the subject and object pronouns. If you like, have students hold up the subject and object pronoun cards from Blackline Master 81.

Objective: Choose the best subject or object pronoun to complete a sentence.

Materials: Blackline Master 83; pencils

[**Answers:** he; him; We; us; They]

Introduce Blackline Master 83: Find the Missing Pronouns

Pair students of varying ability. Give each pair a copy of Blackline Master 83. Read the directions aloud. Then have volunteers read the subject and object pronouns in the word box. Complete the first sentence together. Tell the pairs to read the remaining sentences and choose the best pronoun from the box to fill in each blank. Point out that one pronoun from the word box will not be used.

Informal Assessment

Have students turn to pages 368 and 369, and point to the photographs. Ask: *What subject and object pronouns could you use to describe these people? Tell me what is happening in the pictures. Use subject and object pronouns in your sentences.*

Use the following chart to assess and reteach.

Are students able to:	
identify subject and object pronouns?	Reteach using the Language Support Activity on TE page 340 for oral practice.
choose the best subject or object pronoun to complete a sentence?	Reteach using part A of the meeting Individual Needs Practice page on TE page 341.
use subject and object pronouns correctly in their writing?	Reteach using the Reteach Activity on TE page 341.

Red for Subject/Blue for Object

Cut out the two cards. Color the subject pronoun card red. Color the object pronoun card blue. Hold up the correct card when you hear a pronoun.

subject pronoun

object pronoun

Pronouns and Pictures

Read each sentence. Find the subject pronoun and object pronoun. Write the pronouns on the correct lines under the sentence. Draw a picture to show the meaning of the sentence.

1. I was afraid to try rollerblading until my family helped me.

_____   _____
subject pronoun   object pronoun

2. I wanted to learn to rollerblade, so my mother gave me skates for my birthday.

_____   _____
subject pronoun   object pronoun

3. She took my sisters and me to a skating rink.

_____   _____
subject pronoun   object pronoun

4. Mother helped us put on our skates before we started.

_____   _____
subject pronoun   object pronoun

5. Soon I was skating with my sisters, not just watching them!

_____   _____
subject pronoun   object pronoun

Find the Missing Pronoun

Read the pronouns in the word box. Read each sentence. Choose a subject or object pronoun from the box to complete the sentence. Write the correct pronoun on the line.

Subject Pronouns	he	we	they
Object Pronouns	him	us	them

1. Raoul and Layla wanted to buy a present for their grandfather because

_____ was celebrating his 65th birthday.

2. Grandpa loved gardening, and they wanted to choose

something special for _____ .

3. "_____ can collect money from everyone in our family for the

present," said Layla.

4. "Asking our relatives to help _____ is a great idea" said Raoul.

5. _____ collected enough money

to buy a small magnolia tree for their grandfather.

I. DEVELOP ORAL LANGUAGE
Oral Focus on Grammar Skill

Objective: Orally describe a photograph using indefinite pronouns.

Whole Group Oral Language Activity

Ask students to look at the photograph at the bottom of page 348. Say: *There is a tent by the lake. Do you think anyone is in the tent?* Let students vote by raising their hands to show whether or not they think someone is in the tent. Use indefinite pronouns to describe the results of the vote. *(Several of you think someone is in the tent. Many of you think nobody is in the tent.)*

List on the board the indefinite pronouns you have used so far in your discussion: *anyone, several, someone, many, nobody,* etc. Explain that an indefinite pronoun is a pronoun that does not refer to a particular person, place, or thing.

Invite a student to point to the lake in the photograph. Say: *Someone is swimming in the lake. Is* someone *singular or plural?* (singular) Add four or five more people to your lake and say: *Many are swimming in the lake. Is* many *singular or plural?* (plural). Explain that indefinite pronouns can be singular or plural, but they're not always easy to figure out. *Someone* and *many* are easy. But others need to be memorized. Point out the chart of singular and plural indefinite pronouns on PE page 348. Have volunteers read the words aloud one at a time. As a class, make up an example sentence using each one.

Scaffolded Verbal Prompting

Use the following verbal prompts to help students better understand indefinite pronouns.

Nonverbal Prompt for Active Participation

Pre-Production: *Look at this box. What do you think is in the box? Raise your hand to vote for* something *or* nothing.

One- or Two-Word Response Prompt

Early Production: *Look at this box. Do you think anything is inside it?* (Yes, I think something is in the box. No, I don't think anything is in the box.)

Prompt for Short Answers to Higher-Level Thinking Skills

Speech Emergence: *Look at the photograph on page 348. What do you see?* (Someone is by the tent. Nobody is swimming in the lake.)

Prompt for Detailed Answers to Higher-Level Thinking Skills

Intermediate and Advanced Fluency: *Describe the scene in the photograph on page 348. Use indefinite pronouns.*

II. DEVELOP GRAMMAR SKILLS IN CONTEXT
Visual/Physical Focus on Grammar Skill

Objective: Develop and demonstrate understanding of indefinite pronouns.

Materials: Blackline Master 84; scissors; paper; pencils

Extension: Write the groups' sentences on the board. Read each sentence aloud and have students identify the indefinite pronoun. Ask: *Is it singular or plural?* Read the sentence again. Have students identify the verb. Ask: *Is it singular or plural?* Work together to make any necessary corrections so that all the indefinite subject pronouns agree in number with their verbs.

TPR

Whole Group Activity

Play "Simon Says" using directions that include indefinite pronouns. Explain that the students should follow all commands that begin with the words *Simon says.* If they follow any other commands they will sit down and be out of the game. Since the commands may include indefinite pronouns, students may have to choose when to respond (for example: *Simon says, someone clap your hands.).* Play until just one student is left or until you run out of time.

Small Group Activity

Divide the class into small groups. Have the groups pretend they are camping in the woods. Give each group a card describing something they would need to do while camping (make dinner, put up a tent). Have each group act out the task and let the other groups guess what it is. Then ask the members of each group to think of a way to face their challenge and to describe it in a simple sentence. (We can catch fish. We could make a tent.) Next, have the students in each group replace the subject of their sentence with an appropriate indefinite pronoun. (Many of us can catch fish. Several of us could make a tent.)

Partner Activity

Assign partners of varying levels of fluency. Give each pair a copy of Blackline Master 84, scissors, paper, and pencils. Read the Blackline Master directions together. Have the students cut out the word cards (not the picture cards) and put them facedown in a pile. Show them how to draw a tic-tac-toe grid on their paper. Then let the pairs play Indefinite Pronoun Tic-Tac-Toe. Students take turns drawing a card and identifying the indefinite pronoun as singular or plural. If they are correct, they can mark an X or O on the tic-tac-toe board. The first player to get three marks in a row goes first the next round.

Technology Link

Type the following indefinite pronouns into a word processing program: *someone, several, everybody, nothing, few, many.* Pair students of varying language levels. Have the students type a present-tense verb next to each indefinite pronoun, making sure it agrees in number.

Someone

Several

Everybody

Nothing

Few

Many

III. PRACTICE GRAMMAR SKILLS
Written Focus on Grammar Skill

Use Blackline Masters 85 and 86 to reinforce understanding and use of indefinite pronouns.

Objective: Match sentences containing indefinite pronouns with the pictures they describe.

Materials: Blackline Master 85; pencils; scissors; glue or paste

[Answers: Nothing is in the car.; Everything is in our tent.; Everyone is watching the sunset.; Both of the bear cubs are going into the tent.; Somebody took our food!]

Introduce Blackline Master 85: Making a Story
Distribute Blackline Master 85. Read the directions aloud and discuss them with the class. Have pairs work together to find the indefinite pronouns in the sentences and mark them as singular or plural. Then the partners should cut out the sentences and place them next to the pictures they describe. When they are sure they have the sentences in the right place, they can glue them in the boxes and read the story.

Informal Assessment
Have students turn to page 349 in their textbooks. Read aloud a sentence from More Practice A. Ask student volunteers to identify the indefinite pronoun and tell whether it is singular or plural.

Objective: Identify the verb form that agrees with an indefinite pronoun.

Materials: Blackline Master 86; pencils

[Answers: want; get; rows; pulls; is]

Introduce Blackline Master 86: Verb Agreement
Form student pairs. Distribute Blackline Master 86. Read the directions aloud and talk about them with the students. Remind students that they need to use a plural verb with a plural indefinite pronoun. Invite students to look at the picture under the sentences and to talk about what they see. Then have students work in pairs to finish the activity.

Informal Assessment
Have students turn to page 348, and point to the photo on the page. Ask: *What do you see in this picture? What indefinite pronouns could you use to talk about what you see?*

Use the following chart to assess and reteach.

Are students able to:	
identify indefinite pronouns in sentences?	Reteach using the Meeting Individual Needs Reteach page on TE page 349 for oral practice.
tell whether an indefinite pronoun is singular or plural?	Reteach using part A of the Extra Practice page on TE page 409.
use indefinite pronouns in sentences with verbs that agree in number?	Reteach using the Language Support Activity on TE page 348..

Indefinite Pronoun Tic-Tac-Toe

Cut out the word cards. Tell whether each indefinite pronoun is singular or plural. Mark an X or O on your tic-tac-toe board. Try to get three in a row! Cut out the picture cards. Make sentences using the indefinite pronouns and the pictures. Mark an X or O on your tic-tac-toe board. Try to get three in a row!

anybody	both	many	everyone
several	nobody	someone	each

Name_____ Date_____

Making a Story

Look at the pictures and read the sentences. Find the indefinite pronoun in each sentence. Decide if the pronoun is singular or plural. If it is singular, circle it. If it is plural, underline it. Cut out the sentences. Paste each sentence next to the picture it describes. Read the story!

Everyone is watching the sunset.

Everything is in our tent.

Both of the bear cubs are going into the tent.

Nothing is in the car.

Somebody took our food!

Verb Agreement

Read each sentence. Find the indefinite pronoun. Decide whether it is singular or plural. Circle the verb that agrees with the indefinite pronoun. Read the sentence to your partner. Does it sound correct?

1. Many of the campers want / wants to go fishing.

2. Several of the campers get / gets their fishing poles.

3. Somebody row / rows the boat to the middle of the lake.

4. Something pull / pulls on Antonia's fishing line.

5. Everyone is / are happy because Antonia caught a big fish for dinner.

ROOT WORDS

Introduce this lesson before Pupil Edition pages 368–369.

I. DEVELOP ORAL LANGUAGE
Oral Focus on Vocabulary Skill

Objective: Orally describe a picture and identify word roots.

TPR

Whole Group Oral Language Activity

Ask, *Where would a school play be shown?* (theater; auditorium; on a stage.) Write the word *auditorium* on the board. Ask, *Who watches the play in an auditorium?* (parents; audience) Write the word *audience* on the board as well. Write the root, *aud,* on the board. Explain that a root is a part of a word with a certain meaning, and the root aud, means "to hear." Ask, *What does an audience hear?* (They hear actors in a play.) Ask, *What do you do in an auditorium that has to do with hearing?* (You hear people speak.) Repeat the exercise with the words *script, description,* and *location.*

Scaffolded Verbal Prompting

Use the following verbal prompts to help students better understand root words.

Nonverbal Prompt for Active Participation

Pre-Production: *Look at the picture on page 413. Point to the girl holding a script.*

One-or Two-World Response Prompt

Early Production: *Look at the picture on page 413. What is the girl in the white shirt holding? Use a root world to answer the questions. Tell what the root word means.*

Prompt for Short Answers to Higher-Level Thinking Skills

Speech Emergence: *Describe one student in the picture who is wearing a costume. Did you use any words that might have the same root? What were they?*

Prompt for Detailed Answers to Higher-Level Thinking Skills

Intermediate and Advanced Fluency: *Look at the photo on page 413. What do you think the scene is about? Tell me any root words you might have used.*

II. DEVELOP VOCABULARY SKILLS IN CONTEXT
Visual/Physical Focus on Vocabulary Skill

Objective: List words with similar word roots and describe a personal goal using those words in a sentence.

TPR

Small Group Activity

Organize the class into small groups. Give each group an index card with a root from the list on page 368 written on one side. Ask students to choose a skill they would like to improve, and a root word connected to it. Tell them to act it out while the class tries to guess the word that contains the given root. For example, *I work on my basketball game. Pos (root). I want to play a lot of positions.*

Partner Activity

Pair students of varying language levels. Ask students to think about people who had a problem to solve and took action. Have students refer to the list of roots on page 368 and attempt to use an example of a word containing a given root as they tell about their person. Write a sentence or two on the board from each group that uses a root word. Ask students to come up to the board, underline the word and double underline the root.

Technology Link

Pair students of varying language levels. Type into a word-processing program three words and their root. Have students use the underline feature to highlight and underline the root in each word.

III. PRACTICE VOCABULARY SKILLS
Written Focus on Vocabulary Skill

Practice A

Materials: Blackline Master 87; scissors, glue

[Answers: 1. aud; 2. spect; 3. pos; 4. scribe; 5. loc; 6. dict; 7. port]

Introduce Blackline Master 87: Match Roots to Words

Distribute Blackline Master 87. Read the directions aloud. Remind students to look carefully within each word to find the matching group of letters that form the root. Tell them to cut out the root and paste it in the box next to the word. Have students complete the other matching exercises.

Practice B

Objective: Use Roots to Find the Correct Word to Finish the Sentence

Materials: Blackline Master 88, pencils

[Answers: 1. auditorium; 2. portable; 3. predicted; 4. position; 5. pedaled; 6. spectators]

Introduce Blackline Master 88: Be a Root Detective

Distribute Blackline Master 88. Ask a student volunteer to read the directions. Point out how the meaning of the root can help students guess what the word means. Have students finish the exercise on their own. Encourage students to cross out each word in the box after it has been used in a sentence to help students narrow their choices.

Informal Assessment

Have students turn to page 401 in the textbook. Read a sentence in exercise J. Ask students to name the root of the underlined word. What does the root mean?

Use the following chart to assess and reteach.

Are students able to: identify roots and the words that contain them?	Reteach by using the Language Support Activity on TE page 368.
match roots with their meanings?	Reteach by using the Reteach Activity on TE page 369.

Match Roots to Words

Read each word. Read each root on the right side of the page. Find the root that is found in the word. Cut out the root and paste it in the box next to the correct word.

1.

auditorium	

2.

inspect	

3.

position	

4.

describe	

5.

location	

6.

dictionary	

7.

portable	

dict

scribe

loc

pos

aud

spect

port

Root Word Detective

Read each sentence. Look at the root shown in each sentence. Find the word in the box below that contains the root. Write the word on the line to complete the sentence.

auditorium	position
portable	predicted
reporter	pedaled
spectators	

Example: I was a (port) _____ for the school newspaper.

Sample answer: reporter

1. Everyone met in the (aud) _____ before

the bicycle race.

2. I took a (port) _____ tape recorder to

interview Ariana.

3. Some students (dict) _____ Ariana would

win the race.

4. The racers got into (pos) _____.

5. The racers (ped) _____ their bicycles.

6. The (spect) _____ cheered at the finish line.

Introduce this lesson before Pupil Edition pages 370–371.

I. DEVELOP ORAL LANGUAGE
Oral Focus on Composition Skill

Objective: Orally determine the words of dialogue and identify who is speaking.

TPR

Whole Group Oral Language Activity

Greet the class, *Good morning, class.* Motion for class to respond. (*Good morning,* <u>Teacher's Name</u>). Ask one of the students in the class, "*How are you, (Student's Name)?*" (I am fine/sleepy/hungry.) Invite each student to exchange greetings with their neighbor and encourage their neighbor to respond. Ask, *What are we doing?* (Talking, saying hello) Explain that when we speak to each other, it is called *dialogue.* Explain that in a story, using dialogue—in other words, having your characters talk—is a good way to tell the reader what the character is like.

Scaffolded Verbal Prompting

Use the following verbal prompts to help students better understand how dialogue helps describe a character as part of a story.

Nonverbal Prompt for Active Participation

Pre-Production: *Look at the picture on page 371. Point to the person who might say, "I am wearing a blue raincoat today."*

One- or Two-Word Response Prompt

Early Production: *Look at the picture on page 371. Listen to this quotation: "I'm cold," said the boy in the yellow raincoat. Make up what the person in the blue raincoat might say in return.*

Prompt for Short Answers to Higher-Level Thinking Skills

Speech Emergence: *What might the two people be saying to each other? What is it called when people talk to each other in a story?*

Prompt for Detailed Answers to Higher-Level Thinking Skills

Intermediate and Advanced Fluency: *Look at the picture on page 371. Make up a few lines of dialogue as these two people discuss a challenge they might face.*

II. DEVELOP COMPOSITION SKILLS IN CONTEXT
Visual/Physical Focus on Composition Skill

Objective: To tell a story using dialogue.

TPR

Extension: Ask students to act out their stories, making up a few extra lines of dialogue to extend their quotations into a story.

Small Group Activity

Invite students to sit in a circle and make up a simple story about facing a challenge. Have the students tell the story by using dialogue. Going around the circle, ask them to make up a sentence of dialogue that moves the story along. For example, *"Where is the grocery store?" asked Jose. "It is on the next block," said a policeman.*

Partner Activity

Partner students of varying language levels. Give each pair four cards; each card is numbered and has a short sentence of dialogue written on it. Have students read the cards, underline the words spoken, and draw a picture of the character in the dialogue with a word balloon to indicate speech. Have students write the number of each card in the word balloon and share with the class their picture and the dialogue that matches it.

Technology Link

Type three short sentences of dialogue without punctuation into a word-processing program. Pair students of varying language levels. Ask them to insert the correct quotation marks around the direct quote of the sentence. Include an example for them to follow.

III. PRACTICE COMPOSITION SKILLS
Written Focus on Composition Skill

Introduce Blackline Master 89: Identifying the Dialogue

Objective: Identify the part of the sentence that contains the actual quotation.

Materials Blackline Master 89; crayons

Distribute Blackline Master 89. Read and discuss the directions with the class. Have a student read the first sentence. Ask students to point to the quotation marks and circle them. Have students color the quotation box. Then have the class complete the exercise independently.

Introduce Blackline Master 90: Punctuating Sentences with Dialogue

Objective: Use correct punctuation in sentences with dialogue.

Materials: Blackline Master 90; pencils

Distribute Blackline Master 90. Read the directions aloud. Write the first sentence on the blackboard. Ask, *What is missing?* (punctuation) Ask a student volunteer to come up and punctuate the sentence. Ask pairs to complete the remaining sentences by using the correct capitalization and punctuation.

Informal Assessment

Have students turn to page 371 in their textbooks. Read aloud a sentence from Grammar Link. Ask students to identify the words that the speaker said.

Use the following chart to assess and reteach.

Are students able to: identify the part of the sentence that is the quotation?	Reteach by using Teaching Tip Activity on TE page 370.
punctuate a sentence with dialogue correctly?	Reteach by using the Reteach Activity on TE page 371.

Identifying the Dialogue

Read each sentence. Look at each part within the box. Circle the quotation marks. Color the boxed part of the sentence that is the quotation.

1. | "The flowers are in the vase," | | said Carol. |

2. | "I ate them," | | said Mike. |

3. | Carol said, | | "You are teasing me." |

4. | Mike said, | | "I think I am funny." |

5. | "I think you are annoying," | | said Carol. |

Punctuating Sentences with Dialogue

Read the sentences. Identify the quotation. Punctuate the sentences correctly. Look at the example if you need help.

Did you:

- Put in the quotation marks at the beginning and end of the quotation?
- Capitalize the first word in the quotation?
- Put a comma after the last word in the quotation, before the end quotation mark?
- Put a period at the end of the sentence?

Example: "I want to go to the movies," said Cheryl.

1. You need money to go to the movies said Jorge.

2. I saved money from my birthday said Cheryl.

3. You need a car. It is far said Jorge

4. I called Cousin Abdul. He will give us

a ride said Cheryl.

Introduce this lesson before Pupil Edition pages 374–395.

I. PREWRITE
Oral Warm Up

Objectives:
- Express possible story ideas orally.
- Record story ideas through pictures and words.

TPR

Whole Group Oral Language Activity

Arrange with another teacher or another volunteer to act a scene no more than 2 or 3 minutes long. Enact a simple challenge, such as trying to move a heavy desk a few feet. When you have finished the scene, ask the class, *what happened?* (You moved the desk). *Was it easy or hard to do?* (It was hard.) *How could you tell?* (You were struggling, it took two people, and you had to work together) *Did I move the desk by myself?* (No, a teacher helped you.) *Name one way I tried to move the desk.* (You tried to pick it up.) *Name another way I tried to move the desk.* (You and the other teacher leaned against one side.) List the student responses on the board.

Introduce the Writing Mode

Graphic Organizer

Objectives:
- Begin prewriting to choose a story idea.
- Use a graphic organizer to record ideas.

Materials: Blackline Master 91; crayons

Explain that a story tells about something that happens. It comes from thinking about what *could* happen, or it might resemble something that happened.

A story needs to have action. Model a story about moving the desk. (Example: *I wanted to move my desk, so I asked Mr. Feldman to help me. We tried to move it, but it would not budge. We pushed and pulled. Finally the desk moved. I heard a strange noise "Stop!" I said. A crumpled piece of paper had fallen out of the desk. It was a treasure map!*) Invite volunteers to make up their own story about moving the desk.

Scaffolded Writing Instruction

Pre-Production and Early Production

Have students think of an idea for a story. Using Blackline Master 91, have students draw pictures in the boxes to show a problem, possible actions, and a solution.

Speech Emergence

Ask students to label their pictures with words or short phrases. Have them act out the parts to their story.

Intermediate and Advanced Fluency

Ask students to explain their ideas for a story orally and in writing using full sentences along with pictures to illustrate and clarify their points.

Research and Inquiry: Watch a Documentary Movie

Taking notes while doing research can help you remember useful information. One way of doing research is to watch a documentary. A documentary is a movie that tells a true story about a person or event. It does not use actors, but may use pictures, filmclips or other pieces of evidence. Information in a documentary could help make a story more realistic. Brainstorm topics for possible stories and make a list of facts that could be checked by watching a documentary.

II. DRAFT

Objectives:
- Use sequencing strategies to organize a story.
- Begin drafting a story.

TPR

Focus on Writing a Story

Ask, *what story did we act out?* (Moving a heavy desk.) Ask, *what was one way we might turn the event of moving a desk into a story?* (By thinking about what could happen—even if it is fiction, such as finding a treasure map.) List student responses on the board and then choose one idea to use as a model. Form a circle and tell a group story about meeting this challenge. Encourage students to act out or use words to communicate their ideas.

Scaffolded Writing Instruction

Pre-Production and Early Production

Blackline Master 92: First, Second, Third

Use Blackline Master 92 to help students organize their story into a logical sequence. Divide students into groups of three of varying levels. Have students talk amongst themselves about the order of events in their story idea from Blackline Master 91.

Speech Emergence

Blackline Master 93: Sequence of a Story

Have students draw and label a picture in each circle. In the top, they should draw what happened first and present the problem. In the middle circles, they should show two actions that move the story along. In the last circle, they should draw their solution to the problem and how their story ends. Encourage them to label their pictures and use time-order words to show sequence.

Intermediate and Advanced Fluency

Students should begin writing their own story. Encourage them to put their problem, actions, and solution in a logical order. They should include details about the actions that move the story along.

III. REVISE

Objectives:
- Revise a story by adding details.
- Include descriptive words to make the story more lively.

Focus on Elaboration

Write the following sentences on the board and read them aloud with the class:

I wanted to move my desk.

I asked a friend to help me.

When we moved the desk, we found a map.

Have students think of a word or two for each sentence that adds an important or lively detail. For example, ask: *What was the desk made of?* (wood, metal). *Was it heavy or light?* (heavy) *What was the name of the friend who helped move the desk?* (Answers vary—i.e. Mr. Feldman). *What kind of map was it?* (treasure) *What kind of ring?* (gold, silver, diamond, ruby)

Scaffolded Instruction for Revising

Have students add one or two details in the drawings for Blackline Master 92 to help them understand the idea of elaboration. Encourage students to use color to reinforce the concept.

Use Blackline Master 93 to help students elaborate on their stories. Have them add two details in each drawing and write about them on the line to the right of each circle.

Have students ask partners: *What are one or two details you would like to know about the story?* Encourage students to include more details to add interest to their story.

Technology Link

Pair students of varying levels. Type the following sentence into a word processing program: *I found a map in a desk.* Have students use the cut and paste feature on the pull-down menu under Edit to insert details and revise the sentence.

IV. REVISE • PEER CONFERENCING
Focus on Peer Conferencing

Paired Activity

Objectives:
• Participate in peer conferences.
• Give and receive constructive feedback and suggestions for improvement.
• Revise their story.

Pair pre-production and early-production students with more advanced students. Have more fluent students retell the story following the pictures drawn by the pre- and early-production students. Have the fluent student explain at least one thing he/she liked about the story and give one suggestion to help improve it.

Ask students, *What are some things you should look for in a story?* Using page 389 of the pupil edition, write a checklist on the board for each proficiency level for students to refer to as they conference.

V. PROOFREADING

Focus on English Conventions

Objectives:
• Demonstrate comprehension of proofreading strategies.
• Use subject and object pronouns correctly.

Write the following sentences on the board and ask students what is wrong with them: *Us are going to the park. I like he very much.* Review the use of subject and object pronouns and list examples of these pronouns in separate categories on the board. Ask, *When is a subject pronoun used?* (to substitute for the subject of a sentence). *When is an object pronoun used?* (to substitute for the object of a verb or preposition in a sentence.) Invite student volunteers to correct the two sentences written on the board. Explain that proofreading means looking for mistakes in written work and correcting them.

Objective:
• Choose the correct subject and object pronouns to complete a sentence

Materials: Blackline Master 94, pencils

[Answers for Blackline Master 94: 1. us; 2. They; 3. me; 4. He; 5. him]

Spelling Tip: Have students make lists of rhyming words to help them look for spelling patterns. Have them circle words in their rhyming lists that sound as if they should be spelled with the same pattern as other words in the group, but are spelled differently, for example, *toes, goes* and *grows.*

Divide students in groups of 2 or 3 of varying levels. Encourage students who are at the early stages of learning English to use the pictures next to the sentences to help them read each sentence.

After students have finished Blackline Master 94, have them look at the proofreading checklist on the board. Checking for correct spelling should be a part of the list. Have students look over their stories and ask for the correct spelling of one word. Write these words on the board and keep a running list of words students need help in spelling. When another student asks about a word on the list, find the word on the board and have students practice sounding it out.

Ask a student volunteer to suggest a word he/she would like to check in the dictionary. Write the word on the board. Have another student point to the first letter in the word, and turn to the section for that letter. Then have a student point to the second letter in the word. Explain the strategy of using the second and third letter to find a word.

VI. PUBLISH

Objectives:
• Prepare a final neatly-presented copy.
• Share stories either by reading or explaining them orally using illustrations.

Extension: Have the class work in groups to create a mural illustrating the story of moving the desk and finding a secret treasure map.

TPR

Use page 392 of the Pupil Edition to create a checklist. Organize the checklist so that it applies to students of varying levels: students presenting their stories orally using pictures, and students reading their stories.

Create a Book for Each Story and Display.

Ask student volunteers to present their stories. For students who are less fluent, pair them with a more fluent student who can narrate while the "author" shows his illustrations. Encourage more advanced students to read their stories to the group. Have students bind their stories into individual books and display on shelf. Invite students to draw a picture illustrating the story on the cover.

VII. LISTENING, SPEAKING, VIEWING, REPRESENTING

TPR

Modify the steps on pages 394–395 to generate activities that will focus on the talents and capabilities of all students, including those students in the pre- and early-production stages. Have these students modify ideas so that their presentations are oral or focus primarily on visuals.

Informal Assessment

Base your assessment on how well the students have responded to the different stages of creating a story: for example, ordering their pictures sequentially, making their pictures as detailed as possible, acting out the story line, pointing the appropriate picture at the moment it is being explained.

Record What Is Happening

Think of a problem that needs to be solved and draw or write the problem in the first box. In the middle box, draw or write actions that will reach a solution. In the last box, draw or write how the problem will be solved.

Problem

Action

Solution

First, Second, Third

Think of a story about facing a challenge. In box 1, draw a picture of what happened first. Include your problem. In box 2, draw a picture of what happened next. Include your actions. In box 3, draw a picture of what happened in the end. Include your solution.

1.

First

2.

Second

3.

Third

Name_____ Date_____

Sequence of a Story

Use your story idea of a problem, action, and a solution. In the top circle, draw a picture of what happened first. Label your picture and include a time-order word. In the two middle circles, draw pictures of two actions that move the story along. Include labels and time-order words. In the bottom circle, draw a picture of what finally happened. Include your solution.

First	Later	After a while
Next	Finally	In the end
Then		

Time-order Words   **Details**

_____

_____

_____

_____

_____

_____

_____

_____

Subject/Object Pronouns

Read the sentence. Look at the pronouns in the box. Choose the correct pronoun to complete the sentence. Write the pronoun on the line.

They	**he**	**I**	**He**	**we**
Them	**him**	**me**	**Him**	**us**

1. Kuang's family came to see _____

in America.

2. _____ wanted to stay.

3. Kuang met _____ at school.

4. _____ wanted to learn English

and make friends.

5. I helped _____ learn English.

I. DEVELOP ORAL LANGUAGE
Oral Focus on Grammar Skill

Objective: Orally describe various actions, using adverbs.

Whole Group Oral Language Activity

Write the word *Adverb* on the chalkboard. Then walk quickly around the room. *Ask: What am I doing?* (walking) *How am I walking?* (quickly, fast) Write the adverbs that students offer under the word *Adverb*.

Remind the class that verbs tell what we do, such as *talk* or *jump*. Adverbs tell **how** we do it. For example, we can talk *loudly* or *softly*. Add *loudly* and *softly* to the list of adverbs on the board.

Explain that adverbs can also tell **where** we do something. Point to a place in the room and say: *(Student's name), please stand there.* Then point to a spot closer to you and say: *Now stand here.* Give the whole class these commands: *Look up. Look down.* Add *there, here, up,* and *down* to the list.

Explain that adverbs can tell: **when** we do something. Say to the class: *Now touch your head.* Ask: *Which word told when to touch your head?* (now) Add *now* to the list. Say: *Next, smile at me.* Add *next* to the list.

Invite students to take turns giving commands using adverbs. Add new words to the list.

Scaffolded Verbal Prompting

Use the following verbal prompts to help students better understand adverbs that modify verbs.

Nonverbal Prompt for Active Participation

Pre-Production: *Walk slowly. Now walk quickly.*

One- or Two-Word Response Prompt

Early Production: *Look at the picture of the tree on page 417. Tell how you think the wind is blowing.*

Prompt for Short Answers to Higher-Level Thinking Skills

Speech Emergence: *Look at the picture on page 416. What will these two young people do next? How will they do it?*

Prompt for Detailed Answers to Higher-Level Thinking Skills

Intermediate and Advanced Fluency: *Look at the picture on page 416. Use words that tell* how, where, *or when the people in the picture will do something.*

II. DEVELOP GRAMMAR SKILLS IN CONTEXT
Visual/Physical Focus on Grammar Skill

Objective: Develop and demonstrate an understanding of adverbs that modify verbs

Materials: Blackline Master 95; scissors

Whole Group Activity

Give each student a card with *verb* printed on it and a card with *adverb* printed on it. To make sure students can read the cards, have everyone hold up the verb card and then the adverb card.

Write a sentence on the chalkboard, such as *We quickly walked to school.* Read it aloud. Then tell students you will read it again. Have them hold up the verb card when they hear the verb and the adverb card when they hear the adverb. After they have identified the adverb, discuss whether it tells *how, where,* or *when.*

Continue by writing other sentences on the board that contain an adverb that modifies a verb. Read each sentence aloud and ask students to identify the verb and adverb by holding up the appropriate cards. Then work as a class to decide whether the adverb tells *how, where,* or *when.* (Collect the verb and adverb cards to use in the next lesson.)

Small Group Activity

TPR

Extension: Have each group choose one of its activities to act out for the class. Write the group's sentences on the chalkboard. Ask the other students to identify the adverbs and decide whether they tell how, where, or when.

Have the group members take turns acting out health-oriented activities, such as exercising, brushing their teeth, washing their hands, and so on. They should act out each activity in two ways (for example, *carefully* and *carelessly*). The other group members must decide which approach to the activity is better and then describe the activity in sentences using adverbs. For example: *Brush your teeth carefully. Don't brush them carelessly.* If you wish, have the groups make lists of the adverbs they use.

Partner Activity

Blackline Master 95

[**Answers:** walks quickly; talks softly; barks loudly; sleeps quietly]

Provide each pair with a copy of Blackline Master 95 and scissors. Read and discuss the instructions. Point out that each puzzle has two parts: a verb and an adverb that tells more about the verb. The picture on each puzzle illustrates the verb and adverb. Ask the partners to cut out the puzzles, turn the pieces upside down and mix them up, and then take turns drawing pairs of pieces until they have matched all the verbs with the appropriate adverbs.

Technology Link

Type the three adverbs and the three sentences below into a word processing program. Pair students of different language levels. Have them decide which adverb makes sense in each sentence. They can use the cut-and-paste function to place it there.

yesterday   down   quickly

1. You will read this book.
2. I read it.
3. I could not put it.

III. PRACTICE GRAMMAR SKILLS
Written Focus on Grammar Skill

Use Blackline Masters 96 and 97 to reinforce understanding and use of adverbs.

Introduce Blackline Master 96: Choosing Adverbs

Objective: Add appropriate adverbs to sentences that describe pictures

Materials: Blackline Master 96; pencils

[**Answers:** <u>Yesterday</u> I asked my dad for a puppy.; I said, "I will <u>always</u> feed the puppy.";
"I will walk the puppy <u>outside</u>," I said.; Finally my dad said, "Let's go get a puppy!"]

Remind students that adverbs can tell how, where, or when something is done. Organize the class into pairs of varying language levels. Distribute Blackline Master 96. Read aloud and discuss the directions with students. Encourage pairs to study the pictures and discuss the three adverb choices before deciding which adverb fits into each sentence. Then have the pairs write the word they chose on the line.

Informal Assessment

Have students turn to page 417 in their textbooks. Read aloud a sentence from More Practice B. Ask: *What adverbs would fit into this sentence?*

Introduce Blackline Master 97: Replacing Adverbs

Objective: Replace incorrect adverbs in sentences with adverbs that make sense

Materials: Blackline Master 97; pencils

[**Answers:** slowly = quickly; quietly = loudly; patiently = suddenly; never = often]

Form student pairs. Distribute Blackline Master 97. Explain that each sentence on this page has an adverb, but the adverb does not make sense. The students are to find the incorrect adverb and cross it out. Then they will choose a better adverb from the box and write it on the line. Correct and complete the first sentence together. Ask the pairs to complete the rest of the sentences. Remind them to look at the pictures for help.

Informal Assessment

Have students turn to page 416, and point to the photo on the page. Ask: *What adverbs would describe the waves in this picture? How are they moving?*

Use the following chart to assess and reteach.

Are students able to: identify the adverbs in sentences?	Reteach using the Meeting Individual Needs Reteach page on TE page 417.
identify the verb that each adverb describes?	Reteach using part A of the Meeting Individual Needs Practice page on TE page 417.
choose an adverb that will make sense in a specific context?	Reteach using the Language Support Activity on TE page 416.

Matching Verbs and Adverbs

Cut out the four puzzles. Then cut the puzzle pieces apart on the lines. Turn all the pieces upside down and mix them up. Take turns flipping over two pieces. If the pieces you choose go together, say the verb and adverb together and take the pieces. If they don't go together, turn the pieces upside down again. Continue until all the verbs and adverbs are matched.

walks   quickly

talks   softly

barks   loudly

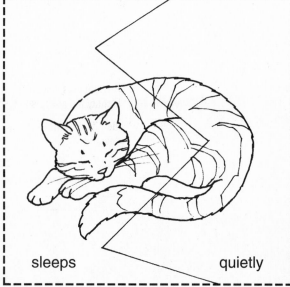

sleeps   quietly

Choosing Adverbs

Look at each picture and read the sentence. Decide which adverb fits into each sentence. Write that adverb on the line.

_____ I asked my dad

for a puppy.

| Never | Yesterday | Tomorrow |

I said, "I will _____

feed the puppy."

| always | never | yesterday |

"I will walk the puppy _____,"

I said.

| here | outside | inside |

_____ my dad said,

"Let's go get a puppy!"

| Often | Never | Finally |

Replacing Adverbs

Look at each picture and read the sentence. Find the incorrect adverb and cross it out. Choose a better adverb from the word box. Write the better adverb on the line.

Word Box			
loudly	often	suddenly	quickly

Reasons to try out for the baseball team:

You slowly learn how to play the game.

Better adverb: _____

Your teammates cheer quietly for you.

Better adverb: _____

You might patiently become a hero!

Better adverb: _____

You never make new friends.

Better adverb: _____

ADVERBS THAT MODIFY ADJECTIVES AND ADVERBS

I. DEVELOP ORAL LANGUAGE
Oral Focus on Grammar Skill

Objective: Orally describe objects and actions, using adverbs that modify adjectives and adverbs.

Whole Group Oral Language Activity

Hold up two identical circles cut out of construction paper. One should be light blue and one dark blue. Ask: *How are these two circles different?* (light blue and dark blue) Write *light blue circle* and *dark blue circle* on the chalkboard.

Remind students that the word *blue* is an adjective. It describes each circle. Write *adjective* above *blue* in both phrases. Explain that the words *light* and *dark* are adverbs. Write *adverb* above these two words. *Light* and *dark* tell what kind of blue the circles are. Point out that adverbs can not only describe verbs, they can also describe adjectives. Invite students to find other examples of light and dark colors in the room and describe them.

Walk very quickly around the room. Point out that you are walking "very quickly" and write that phrase on the board. Then walk at a moderate pace. Explain that you are walking "rather quickly" and write those two words on the board. Ask students to identify the adverbs. (They will probably point out *quickly*.) Then tell them that *very* and *rather* both describe quickly. All four words on the board are adverbs. Adverbs can modify other adverbs as well as modifying verbs and adjectives.

To further demonstrate how adverbs can describe adverbs, ask volunteers to talk very softly and rather softly. Conclude by asking students to name the three kinds of words that adverbs can describe (verbs, adjectives, and other adverbs).

Scaffolded Verbal Prompting

Use the following verbal prompts to help students better understand adverbs that modify adjectives and adverbs.

Nonverbal Prompt for Active Participation

Pre-Production: *Reach very high. Now reach rather high.*

One- or Two-Word Response Prompt

Early Production: *How do you feel when someone gives you a present —very happy or rather happy?*

Prompt for Short Answers to Higher-Level Thinking Skills

Speech Emergence: *Tell me how you feel just before lunchtime.* (Prompt students to include an adverb. Example: *very hungry*)

Prompt for Detailed Answers to Higher-Level Thinking Skills

Intermediate and Advanced Fluency: *Look at the picture on page 419. Tell me what the girl is doing. Now repeat your sentence and add an adverb. What adverb did you use? Does it describe a verb, an adjective, or another adverb?*

II. DEVELOP GRAMMAR SKILLS IN CONTEXT
Visual/Physical Focus on Grammar Skill

Objective: Develop and demonstrate understanding of adverbs that modify adjectives and adverbs

Materials: Blackline Master 98; scissors

Extension: Invite each group to share one or two of its sentences with the class. Write the sentences on the chalkboard. Ask the other students to find the adverb in each sentence that describes an adjective or another adverb.

Whole Group Activity

Give each student a card that says *noun, verb, adverb,* or *adjective.* You might use the verb and adverb cards from the previous lesson. Give each student two different cards, if you wish.

Write a sentence on the chalkboard that includes an adverb modifying an adjective; for example: *A very loud noise scared the dog.* Read the sentence aloud. Ask students to identify the two nouns in the sentence *(noise, dog).* Have two students with noun cards come up and tape the cards above the nouns. Then have the class point out the verb *(scared).* Have someone label it with a verb card. Ask: *Which word tells what kind of noise it was? What is this kind of word called?* Invite a student to label the word *loud* with an adjective card. Ask: *Which word tells how loud it was? What is this kind of word called?* Have a student with an adverb card label *very.* Ask: *Which word does the adverb* very *describe?* (loud) Continue with other sentences that contain an adverb modifying an adjective or adverb.

Small Group Activity

Write two lists on the chalkboard. For one, write adverbs such as *very, too, fairly, so,* and *rather.* For the other, write adverbs and adjectives such as *often, quickly, happily, cold,* and *good.* Have group members match an adverb from the first list with a word from the second. Tell them to think of a sentence that includes those two words.

Partner Activity

Provide each pair with a copy of Blackline Master 98 and scissors. Read and discuss the directions and the adverbs. Point out that this activity requires students to use the adverbs in commands, sentences that tell someone what to do. Then have the pairs complete the activity.

Technology Link

Type three adverbs and three sentences below into a word processing program. Have them decide which adverb makes sense in each sentence. They can use the cut-and-paste function to place it there.

III. PRACTICE GRAMMAR SKILLS
Written Focus on Grammar Skill

Use Blackline Masters 99 and 100 to reinforce understanding and use of adverbs in sentences, and adverbs that modify adjectives and other adverbs.

Introduce Blackline Master 99: Finishing Sentences

Organize the class into pairs of varying language levels. Distribute Blackline Master 99. Read aloud and discuss the directions with students. Encourage pairs to discuss the two adverb choices and pay attention to the picture before deciding which adverb best fits each sentence. Then have the pairs write the adverb they chose on the line and circle the word it describes.

Informal Assessment

Have students turn to page 419 in their textbooks. Read aloud a sentence from More Practice A. Ask students to identify the adverb(s) in the sentence. Then ask them to tell which word each adverb describes.

Introduce Blackline Master 100: Arranging Words

Form student pairs. Distribute Blackline Master 100. Explain that each picture shows a reason why dogs make the best pets. The words below each picture will explain the reason—after students put them into the correct order to make a sentence. Ask the pairs to arrange the words in the right order, write the sentences on the lines, and then circle the adverbs.

Informal Assessment

Have students turn to page 418, and point to the photo on the page. Ask: *How would you describe this frog?* Have the students identify the adverbs in their descriptions.

Use the following chart to assess and reteach.

Are students able to: identify adverbs that modify adjectives and other adverbs?	Reteach using the Language Support Activity on TE page 418.
tell which adjective or adverb an adverb describes?	Reteach using the Meeting Individual Needs Reteach page on TE page 419.
choose the adverb that makes sense in a certain context?	Reteach using the Reteach Activity on TE page 419.

Objective: Choose the best adverbs to complete sentences that describe pictures

Materials: Blackline Master 99; pencils

[**Answers:** We do not have <u>very</u> high buildings.[circle high]; Our roads are <u>usually</u> peaceful.[circle peaceful]; The neighbors are <u>always</u> friendly.[circle friendly]; We <u>almost</u> always eat vegetables right from our garden.[circle always]]

Objective: Arrange words into complete sentences that include adverbs modifying adjectives and other adverbs

Materials: Blackline Master 100; pencils

[**Answers:** (underscored words should be circled) Dogs are <u>always</u> loyal.; Cats are <u>too</u> quiet.; Dogs <u>nearly</u> <u>always</u> protect you.; Dogs <u>rather</u> <u>happily</u> learn tricks or Dogs learn tricks <u>rather</u> <u>happily</u>.]

Using Adverbs

Read the adverbs and cut out the cards. Place the cards in a pile, facedown. Take turns choosing a card. Read the adverb and use it in a command—a sentence that tells your partner what to do. Your partner will follow your command. Continue until you have used all the adverbs in commands.

very	too
rather	quite
almost	completely

Finishing Sentences

Look at each picture and read the sentence. Read the two adverbs under the picture. Decide which adverb fits into the sentence. Write that adverb on the line. Circle the word that the adverb describes.

Reasons why I like living in the country:

We do not have _____

high buildings.

somewhat   very

Our roads are _____

peaceful.

usually   never

The neighbors are _____

friendly.

always   not

We _____ always eat

vegetables right from our garden.

often   almost

Arranging Words

Look at each picture and read the words underneath it. Put the words in order to make a sentence. Write the sentence on the line. Find the adverb in the sentence and circle it. (Some sentences have more than one adverb.)

Reasons why dogs make the best pets:

always are loyal Dogs

_____

too are quiet Cats

_____

you nearly Dogs always protect

_____

learn Dogs rather happily tricks

_____

PREPOSITIONS

I. DEVELOP ORAL LANGUAGE
Oral Focus on Grammar Skill

Objective: Orally describe the positions of objects, using prepositions

Whole Group Oral Language Activity

Write the word *Preposition* on the chalkboard. Say: *(Student's name), please come and stand beside me.* (Help the student stand in the correct place, if necessary.) Say: *Now (student) is beside me.* Write *beside* on the board. Then say: *(Another student), please come and stand behind me.* Write *behind* on the board. Using simple commands, position three other students to illustrate the meaning of *between.* Add that preposition to your list.

Next, use objects and simple commands to illustrate prepositions such as *over/above, under/below, in, on,* and *through.* For example, *Put the pencil on the book. Put the ruler under the desk. Put the eraser in the cup.* Demonstrate each action first, then invite students to follow your commands.

Explain that many prepositions help us describe positions—where things are. Other prepositions tell when or how something takes place *(after supper, until lunchtime, with Betsy).* All prepositions link a noun or pronoun to another word in a sentence. Say a sentence containing a prepositional phrase. Ask students to identify the preposition and the noun or pronoun that follows it. Tell them that they can look at the chart on PE page 428 for a complete list of prepositions.

Scaffolded Verbal Prompting

Use the following verbal prompts to help students better understand prepositions.

Nonverbal Prompt for Active Participation

Pre-Production: *Stand beside your desk. Now stand behind it. Put your hand on your book. Put your hand under your book.*

One- or Two-Word Response Prompt

Early Production: *Where is your desk?* (in the room, in a row, behind his desk)

Prompt for Short Answers to Higher-Level Thinking Skills

Speech Emergence: *Watch me move this pencil. Describe where I put it.* (under a sheet of paper, on a book, and so on)

Prompt for Detailed Answers to Higher-Level Thinking Skills

Intermediate and Advanced Fluency: *Describe the positions of three things in this room. What prepositions did you use?*

II. DEVELOP GRAMMAR SKILLS IN CONTEXT
Visual/Physical Focus on Grammar Skill

Objective: Develop and demonstrate understanding of prepositions.

Materials: Blackline Master 101; scissors

TPR

Extension: Invite each group to demonstrate a preposition for the class, using group members or objects. Ask the other students to name the preposition that is being demonstrated. Point out that an arrangement of objects may illustrate more than one preposition: if a pencil is *on* or *over* a book, the book is also *under* the pencil.

Whole Group Activity

Write a sentence on the chalkboard that includes a preposition, such as: *I see the dog under the table.* Read the sentence aloud. Tell students you will read it again slowly. When you say a preposition, they are to stand up (or raise their hands). Repeat with sentences containing different prepositions. If you wish, have students suggest sentences that include prepositions. Write the sentences on the board, have the "authors" read them aloud, and ask the other students to stand up (or raise their hands) when they hear the prepositions.

Small Group Activity

Write ten or more prepositions on the chalkboard. Challenge each group to select five of them and make up phrases using those prepositions. Then have them work together to draw pictures that illustrate those phrases. Ask them to label each pictures with the prepositions they are illustrating. Provide time or space for the groups to share their pictures with the class.

Partner Activity

Provide each pair with a copy of Blackline Master 101 and scissors. Ask them to cut out the shapes. Then have them take turns using prepositions to direct each other in putting the shapes in certain positions. For example, one partner might say, "Put the circle between the triangle and the star." After following this direction successfully, the other partner will give a direction. Have the pairs continue until they cannot think of any more ways to position the shapes.

Technology Link

Type the three sentences and the prepositions below into a word processing program. Pair students of different language levels. Have them read each sentence. Point out that the underlined preposition is incorrect. Ask them to type over it or backspace and replace it with one of the prepositions in parentheses.

1. The plates are <u>in</u> the table. (on, under)
2. Put a fork <u>under</u> each plate. (beside, through)
3. The soup goes <u>beside</u> the bowl. (over, in)

III. PRACTICE GRAMMAR SKILLS
Written Focus on Grammar Skill

Use Blackline Masters 102 and 103 to reinforce understanding and use of prepositions.

Introduce Blackline Master 102: Filling in the Blanks

Objective: Choose the correct prepositions to complete sentences

Materials: Blackline Master 102; scissors; glue or paste

[**Answers:** We made the cookies <u>with</u> care.; Some <u>of</u> the cookies are hearts.; We put sugar <u>on</u> them.; We baked the cookies <u>for</u> ten minutes.]

Organize the class into pairs of varying language levels. Distribute Blackline Master 102. Read aloud and discuss the directions with students. Have them cut out the prepositions at the bottom of the page. Encourage the pairs to read all the sentences, then try to match each preposition with the correct sentence. When the partners agree that all the sentences and prepositions are correctly matched, they can paste the prepositions in place.

Informal Assessment

Have students turn to page 429 in their textbooks. Read aloud a sentence from More Practice A. Have students find the preposition(s) in the sentence. Ask if students can think of other prepositions that could fit in the sentence.

Introduce Blackline Master 103: Matching Prepositions

Objective: Match prepositions with appropriate sentences

Materials: Blackline Master 103; pencils

[**Answers:** 1. in; 2. on; 3. of; 4. for; 5. to]

Form student pairs, and give each pair a copy of Blackline Master 103. Ask students to read all the prepositions and all the sentences. Then they will work together to draw a line from each preposition to the sentence in which it belongs. If you wish, work as a class to find the correct preposition for the first sentence. Then ask the pairs to match the rest of the prepositions.

Informal Assessment

Have students turn to page 429, and point to the photo on the page. Ask them to describe the pyramids in sentences that include prepositions. To get the students started, you might ask: *What are the pyramids made <u>of</u>? Where are they? What is <u>around</u> them?* Encourage students to identify the prepositions in their sentences.

Use the following chart to assess and reteach.

Are students able to: identify prepositions in sentences?	Reteach using the Meeting Individual Needs Reteach page on TE page 429.
understand the meanings of different prepositions?	Reteach using the Extend Activity on TE page 429.
choose the correct preposition for a certain context?	Reteach using the Reteach Activity on TE page 429.

Using Prepositions

Cut out the shapes. Take turns telling each other where to put two or three of the shapes. For example: *Put the triangle beside the square.* Your partner will follow your direction. Then you can decide if your partner placed the shapes correctly. Continue until you can't think of any more ways to place the shapes.

Filling in the Blanks

Read and cut out the prepositions at the bottom of the page. Look at all the pictures and read the sentences underneath them. Decide which preposition goes in each sentence. Paste that preposition on the line.

Reasons why our cookies are so good:

We made the cookies

_____ care.

Some _____ the

cookies are hearts.

We put sugar _____

them.

We baked the cookies

_____ ten minutes.

of	for	on	with

Matching Prepositions

Read the list of prepositions. Read all the sentences. Decide which preposition fits in each sentence. Draw a line from each preposition to its sentence.

Reasons why people should visit the pyramids:

to

1. The pyramids were built

_____ Egypt long ago.

of

2. They stand _____

the bank of the Nile River.

on

3. They are made _____

heavy stones.

in

4. The pyramids were built

_____ Egyptian kings.

for

5. Would you like to go

_____ Egypt?

PREPOSITIONAL PHRASES

I. DEVELOP ORAL LANGUAGE
Oral Focus on Grammar Skill

Objective: Orally describe the positions of objects, using prepositional phrases

Whole Group Oral Language Activity

Write the words *Prepositional Phrase* on the chalkboard. Put a sheet of paper and a book where students can see them. Hold a pencil in your hand and say: *I am going to put this pencil on...* (Do not finish the prepositional phrase.) Then ask: *Where am I going to put the pencil?*

Guide students to realize that they do not know the answer because you did not complete your sentence. *On* is a preposition, but prepositions must always be followed by a noun or a pronoun. This noun or pronoun is called the *object of the preposition.*

Say: *I am going to put this pencil on the book.* (Do so.) Now ask: *Where did I put the pencil?* (on the book) Ask: *In this sentence, what is the object of the preposition* on? (book) Write *on the book* on the chalkboard.

Pick up the pencil and put it on the paper. Ask: *Where did I put the pencil this time?* (on the paper) *Now what is the object of the preposition on?* (paper) Add *on the paper* to the chalkboard.

Instruct each student to get out a pencil, a book, and a piece of paper. Then give commands for the class to follow; for example: *Put the pencil beside the book. Put the paper under the book. Put the book between the paper and the pencil.* Invite volunteers to give other commands to the class. Add or substitute objects as appropriate.

Scaffolded Verbal Prompting

Use the following verbal prompts to help students better understand prepositional phrases.

Nonverbal Prompt for Active Participation

Pre-Production: *Stand beside your desk. Now sit in your seat. Put your pencil on your book.*

One- or Two-Word Response Prompt

Early Production: *Where is your pencil (notebook, coat, lunch, desk)?* (on my desk, in the closet, by the bookshelf)

Prompt for Short Answers to Higher-Level Thinking Skills

Speech Emergence: *Look at the picture on page 430. Where is the astronaut? What preposition(s) did you use?*

Prompt for Detailed Answers to Higher-Level Thinking Skills

Intermediate and Advanced Fluency: *Describe the positions of three things in this room. What prepositions did you use? What was the object of each preposition?*

II. DEVELOP GRAMMAR SKILLS IN CONTEXT
Visual/Physical Focus on Grammar Skill

Objective: Develop and demonstrate an understanding of prepositional phrases

Materials: Blackline Master 104; common classroom objects

TPR

Extension: Ask the members of each group to make up a sentence that describes one of their pictures. The sentence should include at least one prepositional phrase. Write the sentences on the chalkboard. Invite volunteers to draw one line under each preposition and two lines under the object of each preposition.

Whole Group Activity

Explain that the class is going to play a guessing game. You will give the students a clue about something in the classroom, and they will try to guess what it is. For example, you might say: *I see something yellow that is under something else. What is it?* Make sure that your clue includes a prepositional phrase.

After a student guesses correctly, ask him or her to describe the object in a sentence. *(The yellow book is under the chair.)* Write the sentence on the board. Ask a volunteer to draw a line under the preposition. Have another volunteer draw two lines under the object of this preposition. Continue by giving students other clues involving different prepositions and objects.

Small Group Activity

Give each group a card with a preposition written on it. Then distribute drawing materials and ask each group to draw three pictures. Each picture will show the group's preposition with a different object of that preposition. For example, if the preposition is *on,* the pictures might show an object on a table, on the grass, and on a shirt. Ask the groups to label each picture with the appropriate prepositional phrase, with your help if necessary. Provide time or space for groups to share their pictures with the class.

Partner Activity

Provide each pair with a copy of Blackline Master 104. Read the directions and discuss them together. Explain that each picture shows one or more prepositional phrases. Point out that the first picture shows a dog *on a chair.* Challenge the students to arrange classroom objects to show the prepositional phrase *on a chair.* (For example, a student might sit *on a chair.*) Have the students complete the activity in pairs. Then invite each pair to give the class a TPR command using one of the prepositional phrases from the pictures. (For example: *Sit on a chair. Stand beside a table.*)

Technology Link

Type the two sentences and the prepositional phrases below into a word processing program. Pair students of different language levels. Have them read each sentence and its prepositional phrase. Ask them to use the cut-and-paste function to place the phrases into the sentences. Tell them to read the completed sentences aloud to see if the phrases make sense where they are.

1. I would like to go. (into outer space)
2. I would like to float. (inside a space ship)

III. PRACTICE GRAMMAR SKILLS
Written Focus on Grammar Skill

Use Blackline Masters 105 and 106 to reinforce understanding and use of prepositional phrases.

Introduce Blackline Master 105: Which Is It?

Objective: Choose the correct prepositional phrases to describe pictures

Materials: Blackline Master 105; pencils

[**Answers:** We can go there <u>in</u> a space <u>ship</u>.; We can learn many things <u>on</u> <u>Mars</u>.; Too many people live <u>on</u> <u>Earth</u>.; We have many questions <u>about</u> <u>Mars</u>.]

Organize the class into pairs of varying language levels. Distribute Blackline Master 105, and read aloud the directions. Point out that each picture has two sentences under it, but only one sentence correctly describes the picture. Both sentences have the same preposition, but the object of the preposition is different in each one. Encourage the pairs to read both sentences and circle the correct one. Then have them draw one line under each preposition in the circled sentences and two lines under the objects of the prepositions.

Informal Assessment

Have students turn to page 431 in their textbooks. Read aloud a sentence from More Practice A. Ask students to identify the preposition(s) in the sentence. Then ask them to find the object of each preposition in the sentence.

Introduce Blackline Master 106: Choosing Objects

Objective: Complete prepositional phrases with appropriate objects

Materials: Blackline Master 106; pencils

[**Answers:** I would ride <u>in</u> a space (ship).; Astronauts float <u>through</u> the (air).; I would be famous <u>at</u> my (school).; I might walk <u>on</u> the (moon).]

Form student pairs, and give each pair a copy of Blackline Master 106. Ask students to read the words in the box. Then have them look at each picture and read the sentence underneath. Direct them to underline the preposition. Point out that the object of the preposition is missing. Have the partners work together to choose the correct object of the preposition from the word box and write it on the line.

Informal Assessment

Have students turn to page 431, and point to the photo on the page. Ask students to describe the landing module. To get them started, you might ask: *Where do you think it landed? What is the ground like underneath it? Who might be controlling it?* Encourage them to use sentences with prepositional phrases and to identify the prepositions and objects of the prepositions.

Use the following chart to assess and reteach.

Are students able to: identify the prepositional phrases in sentences?	Reteach using the Meeting Individual Needs Reteach page on TE page 431 for oral practice.
tell which word is the object of a preposition?	Reteach using the Reteach Activity on TE page 431.
draw pictures that correctly illustrate prepositional phrases?	Reteach using the Language Support Activity on TE page 430.

Acting Out Prepositions

Look at the first picture. Decide with your partner what prepositional phrase it shows. Use objects in the classroom to show the same prepositional phrase. Continue with the other three pictures. Some of the pictures may show more than one prepositional phrase.

Which Is It?

Look at each picture and read the two sentences underneath it. Decide which sentence tells about the picture. Circle it. Draw one line under the preposition in that sentence. Draw two lines under the object of that preposition.

Reasons why we should go to Mars:

We can go there in a space ship.

We can learn many things on Mars.

We can go there in a car.

We can learn many things on Earth.

Too many people live on Mars.

We have many questions about Mars.

Too many people live on Earth.

We have many questions about Earth.

Choosing Objects

Look at each picture and read the sentence underneath it. Draw a line under the preposition in the sentence. Find the correct object of the preposition in the word box. Write the object of the preposition on the line.

Word Box			
moon	**school**	**ship**	**air**

Reasons why I want to be an astronaut:

I would ride in a space

_____ .

Astronauts float through the

_____ .

I would be famous at my

_____ .

I might walk on the

_____ .

WORD CHOICE

Introduce this lesson before Pupil Edition pages 454–455.

I. DEVELOP ORAL LANGUAGE
Oral Focus on Vocabulary Skill

Objective: Orally identify words as having positive or negative connotations

Whole Group Oral Language Activity

Write Positive and Negative on the board. Explain that Positive usually describes good things, while Negative is used for bad things. Now say: *He told me to come in. He ordered me to come in.* Say that *told* and *ordered* mean almost the same thing but they create different feelings. Ask: *Which sounds meaner?*(ordered) Write *ordered* under Negative. Ask: *Which sounds nicer?* (told) Write *told* under Positive. Tell students that the words they choose when they write can affect the way their readers feel. Have the class think of other pairs of words that mean the same, but have different connotations, such as: *scent/smell, drag/pull, choose/ grab.* Write them on the board under the appropriate headings.

Scaffolded Verbal Prompting

Use the following verbal prompts to help students better understand how the positive or negative form of a word might affect their audience.

Nonverbal Prompt for Active Participation

Pre-Production: *Show me how you look at something. Now show me how you stare at it.*

One- or Two-Word Response Prompt

Early Production: *Would you rather read a story that was funny—or one that was silly?*

Prompt for Short Answers to Higher-Level Thinking Skills

Speech Emergence: *Show how a character in a story might ask for something. Now show this character would demand something. Which action is more positive—asking or demanding?*

Prompt for Detailed Answers to Higher-Level Thinking Skills

Intermediate and Advanced Fluency: *Let's say a character in a story is always asking questions. Describe that character in a positive, then negative way.*

II. DEVELOP VOCABULARY SKILLS IN CONTEXT
Visual/Physical Focus on Vocabulary Skill

Objective: Be persuasive, using words with positive or negative connotations

Small Group Activity

Choose two or three common decisions, such as whether to try out for a certain sport, or whether to see a certain movie. Assign the same decision to two groups. Have one group think of reasons why someone should do the activity, and the other group think of reasons why NOT to do it. Ask each group to present its reasons. Have the class discuss the words used by each group, and how they affected their presentation.

Partner Activity

Extension: Ask students to describe other pairs' pictures in complete sentences.

TPR

Provide pairs with art materials and a card with two synonyms written on it, one with a positive connotation and one with a negative connotation. Ask the partners to discuss how their two words are the same and different. Then have each partner illustrate one of the words. Ask them to write each word at the bottom of its picture.

Technology Link

Type these two sentences into a word-processing program: *1. I like to (watch, guard) people at the mall. 2. Please (watch, guard) my backpack so no one takes it.* Pair students and have them use the delete or backspace keys to choose the appropriate word for each sentence.

III. PRACTICE VOCABULARY SKILLS
Written Focus on Vocabulary Skill

Introduce Blackline Master 107: Which Words Go Together?

Objective: Identify words with similar meanings but different connotations

Materials: Blackline Master 107; pencils

Distribute Blackline Master 107. Read aloud and discuss the directions with students. Tell students that they are to draw lines to connect the pictures that are almost the same. After students match the pictures, help them read the sets of words and identify which word is positive and which is negative.

Introduce Blackline Master 108: Making Word Choices

Objective: Complete sentences by choosing the words with the appropriate connotations.

Materials: Blackline Master 108; pencils

Give pairs a copy of Blackline Master 108. Read and discuss the instructions with students. Explain that they will have to use the picture and the sentence to choose the most appropriate word. After the pairs complete the sentences, ask volunteers to read each one. Ask a different student to explain why that word choice is correct for this sentence.

Informal Assessment

Have students turn to Practice Exercise A on page 455 in the textbook. Read aloud Sentence 3 and ask: *Which word should be used in this sentence?* Point out that the word *amused* indicates that this sentence is positive, so the positive word *outgoing* is correct here. Ask students to think of a sentence for which *loud* would be appropriate. Encourage students to think of a sentence in which the more negative word, *loud,* would be appropriate.

Use the following chart to assess and reteach.

Are students able to:	Reteach by using the Language Support Activity on TE page 454.
identify words with positive and negative connotations?	
choose the correct connotation to use in specific situations?	Reteach by using the Reteach Activity on TE page 455.

Which Words Go Together?

Look at the pictures on both sides of the page. Draw a line from each picture on the left to the picture on the right that means almost the same. Read the words under each set of pictures.

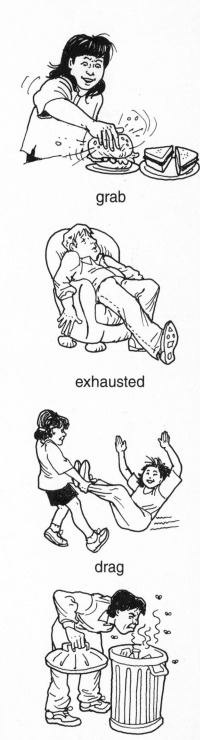

pull

grab

smell

exhausted

choose

drag

tired

stink

Making Word Choices

Decide whether each picture shows something positive or something negative. Decide which word choice is positive and which is negative. Write the word that matches the sentence and the picture on the line.

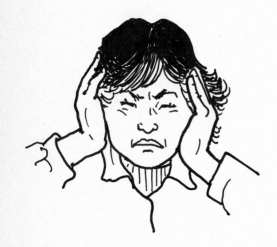

1. The music was almost _____.

deafening   loud

2. My sister has always been _____.

curious   nosy

3. The soup tasted _____.

weird   different

4. It was a _____ day.

quiet   boring

LEADS AND ENDINGS

Introduce this lesson before Pupil Edition pages 456–457.

I. DEVELOP ORAL LANGUAGE
Oral Focus on Composition Skill

Objective: Orally recognize and suggest interesting ways to begin and end a story

Whole Group Oral Language Activity

As a class, brainstorm possible persuasive topics for a story about the picture on page 457. (Examples: why dogs make the best pets, why everyone should have a pet.) Choose a topic and write it on the board. Then have students think of a sentence to begin this story. Explain that this first sentence is called a "lead" because it leads readers into the story. It should persuade readers that the story will interest them. Ask students to think of several leads. Write them on the board.

Now ask students to pretend they have written the story and need an ending. Tell them the last sentence should repeat their most important reason, and let readers know that this is the end of the story. Write several of the students' best ending suggestions on the chalkboard.

Scaffolded Verbal Prompting

Use the following verbal prompts to help students focus on the beginnings and endings of stories and articles.

Nonverbal Prompt for Active Participation

Pre-Production: *Which is a better beginning for a story?* Dogs are good pets. *or:* Would you like to have a friend who is always glad to see you?

One- or Two-Word Response Prompt

Early Production: *Look at the picture on page 457. Tell me one thing that you think people would like to know about the dog or the boy.*

Prompt for Short Answers to Higher-Level Thinking Skills

Speech Emergence: *What interests you about the picture—and might interest other people?*

Prompt for Detailed Answers to Higher-Level Thinking Skills

Intermediate Fluency: *Tell me a lead that would be an interesting way to begin this story.*

II. DEVELOP COMPOSITION SKILLS IN CONTEXT
Visual/Physical Focus on Composition Skill

Objective: Create interesting leads and effective endings to go with stories related to magazine pictures

TPR

Small Group Activity

Give each group newspaper or magazine pictures to use as the basis of a persuasive article. Have the groups think of something to persuade their readers to do, based on a picture from a magazine or newspaper. Then ask each group to think of at least two leads and two endings for its article and write each one on a sentence strip. Have each group display its picture to the class and show the strips with the leads and endings. Have the audience choose those strips they think are leads and those they think are endings.

Partner Activity

Extension: Ask pairs to write their article, putting their ideas into sentences and adding more details. Post the finished articles and encourage students to read each other's articles to learn about fun school and community activities.

Have partners outline an article persuading other students to try a school or community activity. Their outlines should include a lead, two or three important reasons to try the activity, and an ending. When the outlines are ready, form groups so each set of partners can share its lead, reasons, and ending.

Technology Link

Have each group type its brainstormed leads and endings into a word-processing program. Then encourage students to use the cut-and-paste, delete, insert, and other editing features to revise their leads and endings until they are as clear and as interesting as possible.

III. PRACTICE COMPOSITION SKILLS
Written Focus on Composition Skill

Introduce Blackline Master 109: Interesting Readers

Objective: Identify which of two leads and two endings is stronger

Materials: Blackline Master 109; pencils

Pair students with different language levels and distribute Blackline Master 109. Read and discuss the directions. Urge the pairs to discuss both choices for leads and both choices for endings before selecting the stronger ones. If necessary, do the exercises as a class, with volunteers reading the choices aloud and partners making their own decisions.

Introduce Blackline Master 110: Convincing Choices

Objective: Determine if a statement is a lead or an ending.

Choose the more convincing and effective leads and endings

Materials: Blackline Master 110; pencils

Pair students and distribute Blackline Master 110. Read aloud and discuss the directions with students. Read each statement aloud. Ask volunteers to state examples of word clues that help determine if a statement is a lead or an ending. If necessary, do the exercises as a class, with volunteers reading the choices aloud and partners making their own decisions.

Informal Assessment

Have students turn to page 457. Read aloud Sentence 2 in Practice A. Ask: *Is this a lead or an ending?* (ending) *What do the words above all suggest?* (a conclusion or ending) Read aloud Sentence 3 from Practice A and ask: *Is this a lead or an ending?* (lead) *How can you tell?* (A lead invites you to read on; an ending sums things up.)

Use the following chart to assess and reteach.

Are students able to: distinguish a lead from an ending?	Reteach by reviewing Practice A on page 457.
select a stronger lead and ending from two choices?	Reteach by using the MINS Reteach Activity on page 97.

Interesting Readers

Look at each picture. Read the choices underneath. For each picture, underline the lead and the ending that you think is stronger.

A.

Leads:

    1. A head injury can hurt.

    2. Are you too cool to wear a bike helmet?

Endings:

    1. Wearing a bike helmet is cool—and it can save you a lot of pain.

    2. Helmets make riding bikes safer.

B.

Leads:

    1. Will this brook still be here ten years from now?

    2. Brooks are pretty.

Endings:

    1. We must save our brooks.

    2. By caring for our environment, this brook will be around for future children to enjoy.

C.

Leads:

    1. Libraries need a lot of help.

    2. "We couldn't keep the library open without volunteers," says Judy Smith.

Endings:

    1. When you help the library, you help yourself.

    2. Helping at the library is fun.

Convincing Choices

Look at each picture. Read the choices beside it. Determine which statements are leads and which are endings. Write *lead* or *ending* on the line. Underline the lead and the ending that you think is stronger.

A.

_____

_____

1. Donate to the food drive.

2. Bring in a can of food every day that you eat.

3. Many people in our state do not get enough to eat.

4. Do you think you're hungry? You aren't, not really!

B.

_____

_____

1. Do you really need your teeth?

2. It's important to keep your teeth clean.

3. Brush your teeth at least twice a day.

4. Life is much harder without teeth. Do your body a favor and brush.

C.

_____

_____

1. Remember: not everything on the Web is true.

2. Find out the source of Web information before you use it.

3. Would a web site lie to you?

4. You must be careful in using information from Web sites.

WRITING PROCESS

Introduce this lesson before Pupil Edition pages 460–481.

I. PREWRITE
Oral Warm Up

Objectives:
- Respond to a thoughtful question
- Use details, examples, or experiences to support an opinion

TPR

Whole Group Oral Language Activity

Show students a picture of an exotic animal that some people keep as a pet, such as a boa constrictor, monkey, or lion. Ask: *What is this animal called? Should people be allowed to keep this animal as a pet?* Write two headings on the board, such as "Monkeys make good pets" and "Monkeys do not make good pets." Ask students to suggest points that you can write under each heading. (Examples for pro: *Monkeys are smart; they can learn tricks.* Examples for con: *Monkeys get into trouble; monkeys are messy and noisy.*) Have students vote on the monkey question. Ask them which reasons persuaded them to vote the way they did.

Introduce the Writing Mode

Explain to students that they have been trying to see which argument is stronger. In *persuasive writing*, we try to get others to agree with us. Using the reasons on the board, model a persuasive argument. (Example: *Monkeys make good pets. They are cute and smart. They can learn tricks. Some people think monkeys get into too much trouble. You can avoid this problem if you keep them in a cage when you are not home. If you get a monkey for a pet, it will become your best friend.*)

Graphic Organizer

Objectives:
- Begin prewriting for a persuasive article
- Use a graphic organizer to organize ideas

Materials: Blackline Master 111; pencils

Pre-Production and Early Production

Speech Emergence

Intermediate and Advanced Fluency

Scaffolded Writing Instruction

Distribute a copy of Blackline Master 111 to all students. Ask them to think about this question: "Which animal makes a better pet, an iguana or a puppy?"

Have students draw both animals in the top box. Have them draw two reasons why puppies make good pets in one box, and two reasons why iguanas make good pets in the other. Have them draw their answer in the bottom box.

Ask students to draw the pictures as directed and label them with words or phrases.

Have students write sentences that state the question, explain two reasons why each animal makes a good pet, and answer the question.

Research and Inquiry: Search On-Line

Model doing an on-line search for information about a pet. Narrow the search by entering, for example, "iguana + pet." After checking reliable sites, they can print the information they need.

II. DRAFT

Objectives:
- Continue organizing ideas for a persuasive piece
- Begin the first draft of persuasive writing

Focus on Persuasive Writing

Model the process of organizing ideas for persuasive writing. Write each of the sentences below on a separate card. Then read each card aloud, in random order. Ask students to identify the sentence that contains the question to answer. Tape that card high on the chalkboard. Then have students arrange the remaining sentences in a logical order. Remind them to put the strongest argument last. The very last sentence will be the answer to the question. Students might put the sentences in the order below or another order that makes sense. Then have them discuss whether the order makes sense, and if it helps to answer the question.

Which is a better pet—a goldfish or a cat?
Cats sleep all the time.
Sometimes cats ignore you.
Goldfish are fun to watch.
If you forget to feed goldfish sometimes, they will still be okay.
Goldfish do make better pets.

TPR

Pre-Production and Early Production

Blackline Master 112: Here's Why

Scaffolded Writing Instruction

Have students use Blackline Master 112 to support their opinions. Ask them to make drawings or find magazine pictures that illustrate three reasons for their opinions.

Speech Emergence

Blackline Master 113: Explaining Ideas

Use Blackline Master 113 to help students begin their persuasive writing. Have them choose a lead and an ending that best matches the pet they have selected. Then have them draw and label three reasons in the boxes that tell why they feel that pet is best.

Intermediate and Advanced Fluency

Students may begin composing their persuasive writing piece. First, you might review the features of persuasive writing on pages 464 and 465. Have students work together to complete the "reasons" sentences and then write a lead and an ending.

III. REVISE

Objectives:
- Revise a persuasive writing piece
- Add details to elaborate

Focus on Elaboration

Write the following sentences on the board and read them aloud to the class: *Everyone should have a puppy. Puppies like to play.* Review what an opinion is with the students. Ask them which of these sentences is an opinion. Remind them that their opinions need to be supported by convincing reasons. Have volunteers elaborate on each sentence by adding details that help the reader understand the reasons for each opinion.

Scaffolded Instruction for Revising

Pre-Production and Early Production
Blackline Master 112

Use students' work on Blackline Master 112 to help them understand elaboration. Ask them to add details to their pictures to clarify their reasons.

Speech Emergence
Blackline Master 113: Explaining Ideas

Ask students to add words and phrases to their work on Blackline Master 113 to make their leads, reasons, and endings more convincing and complete.

Intermediate and Advanced Fluency

Students may elaborate on the persuasive writing piece they have started by adding details that help convince readers that their opinion is correct.

Technology Link

Have partners print a hard copy of their persuasive writing. Many people find it easier to see problems in a printed copy. Students can mark changes on the paper and then delete and insert them on the screen.

IV. REVISE • PEER CONFERENCING

Focus on Peer Conferencing/Paired Activity

Objectives:
• Participate in peer conferences
• Give and receive constructive feedback
• Revise a piece of persuasive writing

For the peer conferences, pair pre-production and early-production students with more advanced students. Have the more fluent students explain what they see in the other students' illustrations. The pre- and early students can explain what they want to say in their native language. The more fluent students can help supply the appropriate English vocabulary words.

Using page 475 as your guide, prepare a checklist for each proficiency level and write each list on the chalkboard. Then students may refer to them during peer conferences.

V. PROOFREADING

Focus on English Conventions

Objectives:
• Demonstrate proofreading strategies
• Use adverbs and prepositional phrases to elaborate on ideas

Say this sentence: *Iguanas make good pets.*

Ask: *Is this an interesting sentence? Why or why not?* Remind students that adverbs and prepositional phrases can add interest and information to their writing. "Bare" sentences are not very persuasive. Invite students to suggest words and phrases that would make this sentence clearer and more interesting. (Examples: *Iguanas are lively and unusual pets. Iguanas make good pets because they are easy to care for.*)

Objective: Expand sentences with adverbs and prepositional phrases

Materials: Blackline Master 114, pencils

[Answers: 1. Having a puppy <u>in your house</u> is lots of fun.

2. A puppy will sit <u>by the door</u> and wait for you.

3. Iguanas look like <u>very small</u> dinosaurs.

4. Iguanas eat <u>only green</u> plants.]

Spelling Tip: Have students keep sets of sentences for homophones that give them trouble.

Ask students to complete Blackline Master 114 for extra practice on the grammar skill. Then they can look at their own work and identify places where they can add interest with adverbs and prepositional phrases.

After students have completed Blackline Master 114, explain that proofreading includes correcting spelling mistakes. Remind students that some English words sound the same as others, but are spelled differently and have different meanings (homophones). Write a set of sentences on the board to help students differentiate between the two words. For example: *I am going <u>to</u> the store. I will buy <u>two</u> loaves of bread. Will you come, <u>too</u>?*

Also, remind students that words are listed alphabetically in a dictionary. Ask: *Where would you find* to, two, *and* too—*toward the front, in the middle, or toward the end of a dictionary.* (end) *What about* know *and* no*?*(middle) *What about* bare *and* bear? (front)

VI. PUBLISH

Objective:
• Present a neat final copy of a persuasive piece of writing and use a checklist to assess it.

TPR

Extension: If possible, videotape students practicing their presentations. Invite them to review the tapes and identify both strong points and areas they need to strengthen.

Using page 478 as your guide, prepare a checklist for each proficiency level and write these on the chalkboard. Students can then refer to these lists as they prepare the final version of their persuasive writing piece.

Create and Present a Multimedia Report
Organize groups of four students with varying language levels. Have students help each other think of different forms of media, such as pictures, sound, or video, that could add interest and information to their persuasive writing pieces.

VII. LISTENING, SPEAKING, VIEWING, REPRESENTING

Adapt the steps on pages 480–481 to generate activities that will bring out the talents of all students, including those in the pre- and early-production stages. For example, students who are just developing fluency might present much of their report through charts and others visuals rather than explaining all points orally.

TPR

As students present their reports, encourage all listeners to comment on what they heard and to note whether they agree with the speaker's main points.

Informal Assessment
When assessing students' learning, be flexible and encourage students to respond according to their language levels. For example, instead of the traditional answers to writing prompts, you may want students to draw a picture or pantomime a response. Look for evidence in their pictures and actions that show their opinions and reasons.

Getting Organized

In the top box, draw a puppy and an iguana. In the "Puppy" box, draw two reasons why puppies make good pets. In the "Iguana" box, draw two reasons why iguanas make good pets. In the bottom box, draw the animal that you think makes the better pet—a puppy or an iguana.

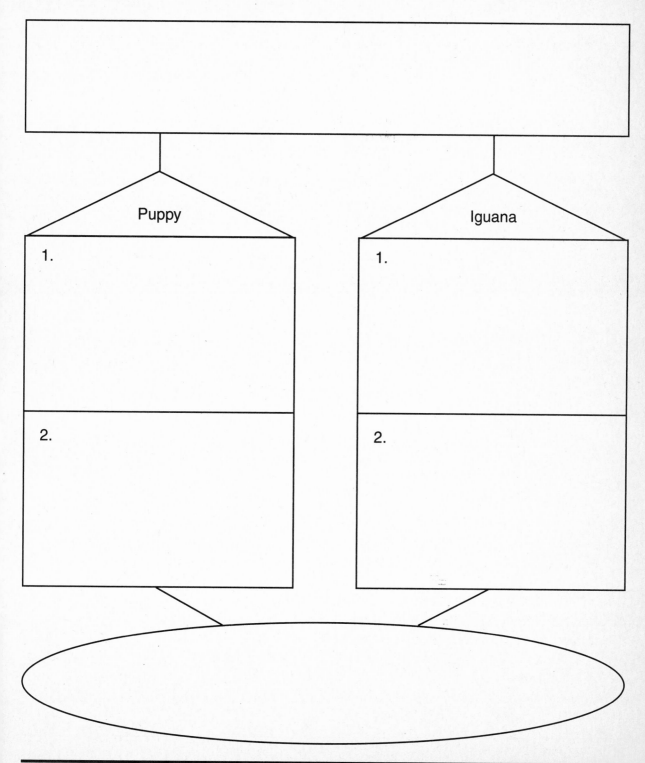

Here's Why

You have already decided whether a puppy or an iguana makes a better pet. Think of three reasons why you are right. Draw or find pictures to show your reasons. Put your pictures in the spaces below.

I think a _____ is best.

Reason 1:

Reason 2:

Reason 3:

Explaining Ideas

Choose a lead that best matches your opinion. Draw pictures or write words that give three reasons to support your opinion. Choose an end that best sums up your opinion.

Lead

1. A puppy can be a warm and fuzzy part of your life.
2. An iguana is like having a miniature dinosaur for a pet.

Reasons

1.

2.

3.

Ending

1. A puppy will be your friend for life!
2. If you like the unusual, choose an iguana.

Adding Interest

Read the words and phrases in the Word Box. Look at each picture and read the sentence. Add a word or phrase to each sentence. Write the new sentence on the line. Read your new sentences to make sure they make sense.

Word Box			
in your house	**by the door**	**very small**	**only green**

1. Having a puppy is lots of fun.

_____

2. A puppy will sit and wait for you.

_____

3. Iguanas look like dinosaurs.

_____

4. Iguanas eat plants.

_____